DevOps for SharePoint

With Packer, Terraform, Ansible, and Vagrant

Oscar Medina
Ethan Schumann

Apress®

DevOps for SharePoint

Oscar Medina
Lafayette, CA, USA

Ethan Schumann
Frisco, TX, USA

ISBN-13 (pbk): 978-1-4842-3687-1
https://doi.org/10.1007/978-1-4842-3688-8

ISBN-13 (electronic): 978-1-4842-3688-8

Library of Congress Control Number: 2018961417

Managing Director, Apress Media LLC: Welmoed Spahr
Acquisitions Editor: Joan Murray
Development Editor: Laura Berendson
Coordinating Editor: Jill Balzano

Cover image designed by Freepik (www.freepik.com)

Distributed to the book trade worldwide by Springer Science+Business Media New York, 233 Spring Street, 6th Floor, New York, NY 10013. Phone 1-800-SPRINGER, fax (201) 348-4505, e-mail orders-ny@springer-sbm.com, or visit www.springeronline.com. Apress Media, LLC is a California LLC and the sole member (owner) is Springer Science + Business Media Finance Inc (SSBM Finance Inc). SSBM Finance Inc is a **Delaware** corporation.

For information on translations, please e-mail rights@apress.com, or visit http://www.apress.com/rights-permissions.

Apress titles may be purchased in bulk for academic, corporate, or promotional use. eBook versions and licenses are also available for most titles. For more information, reference our Print and eBook Bulk Sales web page at http://www.apress.com/bulk-sales.

Any source code or other supplementary material referenced by the author in this book is available to readers on GitHub via the book's product page, located at www.apress.com/9781484236871. For more detailed information, please visit http://www.apress.com/source-code.

Printed on acid-free paper

I dedicate this book to my wonderful wife and daughter and our little puppy, Ginger. I am truly blessed to have you all in my life.

—Oscar

Everything I do is with my amazing wife, Diana, in mind. Thank you for continuous love and support!

—Ethan

Table of Contents

About the Authors

Oscar Medina is an independent consultant with over 18 years in the technology sector. Oscar's experience dates back to the dot-com boom era, where he managed ecommerce sites based on Unix and written in Java. He is an advocate for DevOps practices with a focus on cloud-agnostic tools and modern frameworks. Oscar's software development, coupled with cloud infrastructure, has been instrumental in helping companies realize the benefits of many clouds by mentoring teams in migrating legacy monolithic applications into microservices, building CI/CD pipelines, and orchestrating Docker containers using Kubernetes on three of the leading clouds (AWS, GCP, and Azure), all while maintaining a cloud-agnostic strategy.

Ethan Schumann is a solutions architect for Onica, a leading AWS cloud consulting partner. He specializes in automation and DevOps transformations, with a focus on enterprise implementations using cloud native services and modern tooling. He has experience designing and implementing various technologies, such as Kubernetes containerization, CI/CD constructs for various development workflows, and large-scale Microsoft products, including SharePoint.

About the Technical Reviewers

Jon Hawkesworth is a software engineer at M*Modal Ltd., where he discovered a passion for automating Windows using Ansible. He has twice spoken at AnsibleFest London about Ansible's Windows support. He has contributed several Ansible Windows modules, and he has been an external core committer to the Ansible project since 2016. He can be found helping others automate on the #ansible IRC channel or on the Ansible-project Google group.

Nic Jackson is a developer advocate and polyglot programmer working for HashiCorp. He is the author of *Building Microservices with Go* (Packt Publishing, 2017), a book that examines the best patterns and practices for building microservices with the Go programming language. In his spare time, Nic coaches and mentors at Coder Dojo, teaches at Women Who Go and GoBridge, and speaks and evangelizes good coding practices, processes, and techniques.

Acknowledgments

I'd like to thank two wonderful people that supported me on this journey.

First, Jon Hawkesworth for all of his enthusiasm and dedication on our project. Jon, you made this project so much easier, and I am forever grateful for our friendship.

I'd also like to thank my good friend Nic Jackson at HashiCorp. Nic, I value your friendship and appreciate all the work you put into our project. Your support means so much to me. Thank you for being such a great soul.

—Oscar Medina

CHAPTER 1

Introduction

Before we begin exploring the modern DevOps practices in deploying and managing SharePoint, you need to understand what DevOps is.

In this chapter, we discuss DevOps. We put it into context as it relates to SharePoint infrastructure projects, and how we can leverage these practices and tools to ultimately achieve agility, predictability, repeatability in deployments, and cost savings in the maintenance aspect of the platform on-premises or in the cloud.

Note This book focuses on DevOps as it relates to the infrastructure of SharePoint; however, these principles apply to the development of new features on top of SharePoint (i.e., WebParts, workflows, or new components using the SharePoint Framework).

What Is DevOps?

It is common for the community to have a different interpretation of DevOps. To be clear, DevOps is not a set of tools or a role within the enterprise.

DevOps is comprised of principles (both technical and cultural) and practices for delivering applications and services at high velocity. In many organizations, these practices entail that the development and IT pros/operations teams work together in the full life cycle to achieve this. This is where the cultural aspect of DevOps practice comes into play, as it represents a shift from the traditional silos of these teams; however, the collaboration between these teams is paramount to increase DevOps maturity within the enterprise.

© Oscar Medina, Ethan Schumann 2018
O. Medina and E. Schumann, *DevOps for SharePoint*, https://doi.org/10.1007/978-1-4842-3688-8_1

This collaboration between the two teams increases agility and transparency in delivering the solutions that ultimately both teams are responsible for. With this transparency, product managers and other internal customers can easily gain insight into any progress and/or problems in the delivery pipeline.

Figure 1-1 shows you where three common siloed enterprise teams' efforts are joined to practice DevOps.

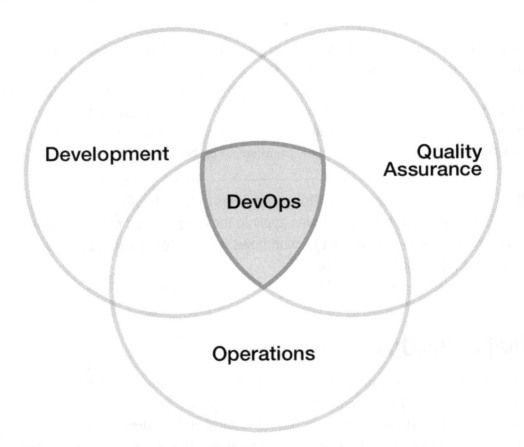

Figure 1-1. *Three traditionally siloed enterprise teams are joined to practice DevOps within the enterprise*

Depending on the size of an organization, there could be fewer teams; for example, an organization may have a development team that writes their own automation tests, and an operations team whose focus is on infrastructure on-premises or in the cloud.

Let's take a closer look at the core practices of DevOps to further help us understand why DevOps is important as it relates to SharePoint initiatives.

DevOps Core Practices

In the scenario shown in Figure 1-2, there are two teams. The development team's focus as it relates to applying the core DevOps practices typically involves code build, test coverage, packaging, and deployment readiness. For the operations team, however, most of the focus is on enabling the automation of the development team's tests and builds, as well as the infrastructure, which includes provisioning, configuration management, orchestration and deployment of software, and infrastructure using IaC (Infrastructure as Code).

Note   We go over IaC in the "Applying DevOps Practices" section of this chapter.

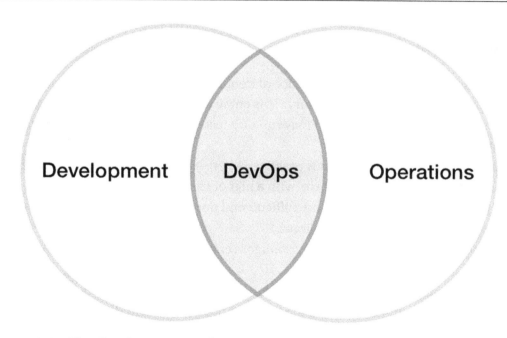

Figure 1-2. *The development and operations teams collaborate to practice DevOps*

It is important to note that the same underlying methods, such as version control, rollback, and testing are used by both teams while applying DevOps practices. Figure 1-3 is a holistic DevOps view that shows the various components—such as continuous integration, continuous delivery, and continuous deployment— throughout various stages in a pipeline.

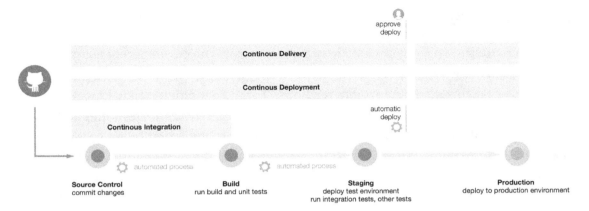

Figure 1-3. *A holistic view of DevOps in the software and infrastructure release process*

Continuous Integration

Continuous integration (CI) is the practice of frequently integrating new code into the overall solution or central repository. This entails automation, typically using a build service such as Jenkins, which may run unit tests and end-to-end tests prior to integration.

This is far different from previous practices where a developer might merge code after extensive changes and, of course, with a higher likelihood of errors and failed builds. In return, this made it far more difficult and onerous to deliver new features, as it took longer to find and address the issues.

With continuous integration, every change is committed and triggers automated build and testing.

There are many benefits to continuous integration, such as improving developer productivity, finding bugs and addressing them more quickly, and delivering new features more frequently.

Continuous Delivery

Continuous delivery (CD) is the practice of having code changes automatically built, tested, and prepped for production release. Continuous delivery takes over where continuous integration ends. In other words, continuous delivery further progresses through the release cycle to deliver the new code and deploy to either a test or a production environment. Continuous delivery ensures that you always have a production-ready, versioned artifact that has gone through the entire testing and build phase.

Continuous Deployment

With continuous deployment, all code changes are automatically deployed to production. This happens after running through the automated build and testing, of course.

DevOps Core Values

In 2010, Damon Edwards and John Willis described DevOps using the acronym CAMS, which stands for culture, automation, measurement, and sharing. The adoption of these values is essential for ensuring success within an organization.

Culture

Indeed, DevOps is about a cultural shift, and it is an undertaking for any organization. It is not just about the tools or toolchain being used. As mentioned earlier, the mere action of bringing together two teams that were previously disconnected and working in silos is a fundamental shift for any enterprise. A collaborative, cross-team problem-solving approach is critical.

Automation

Any organization that has adopted DevOps practices will most definitely say that automation plays a big role. In fact, it is a must-have or prerequisite when it comes to getting things done. This allows the team to focus on the product vision and overall innovation, rather than manually working on repetitive tasks.

Measurement

Incorporating feedback and providing visibility is fundamental when applying DevOps practices. Every possible component that can be measured should be, and sharing those metrics is critical in providing the visibility needed to make educated decisions, which may come from the business, development, and operations teams.

Sharing

Sharing metrics and other information across teams is a key component in cross-team collaboration. It also helps build trust across teams. This is part of that culture shift that we talked about earlier in this chapter. Adopting a sharing culture is perhaps one of the greatest challenges that enterprise-level environments face today, and it is one that must be incorporated to ensure success.

DevOps Tools of the Trade

To practice DevOps, we must rely on modern tooling to allow automation and streamlining of the entire software release cycle. Let's go over key open source tools that help us in the deployment, update, and configuration management of a SharePoint farm.

Tip   In upcoming chapters, we go through step-by-step exercises that use these tools in deploying and updating a SharePoint farm.

Infrastructure as Code

Until recently, the same software development methodology, including source control for a typical software project, has not been applied to infrastructure. As mentioned earlier, the operations team now also treats everything as code and leverages versioning when applying DevOps practices, in addition to automation, as one of the core values of DevOps. We use *Infrastructure as Code* (IaC) to provision SharePoint farms. The same code can be used to provision staging, testing, and production environments to multiple target environments, such as Azure, Amazon Web Services (AWS), or on-premises.

Note   A core component of DevOps is treating infrastructure as code, very much the same as a software development workflow, which includes source control, code, build, test, and maintenance of infrastructure.

Introducing Terraform

To provision or deploy a SharePoint farm and deploy to AWS and Azure, we use HashiCorp's Terraform open source tool. HashiCorp describes Terraform as follows: "Terraform enables you to safely and predictably create, change, and improve production infrastructure. It is an open source tool that codifies APIs into declarative configuration files that can be shared amongst team members, treated as code, edited, reviewed, and versioned." (`www.terraform.io`).

Simply put, Terraform is a tool for building, changing, and versioning infrastructure for popular service providers such as AWS, Azure, OpenStack, and others. It manages low-level components, such as compute instances, storage, and networking. It also manages high-level components, such as DNS entries and other SaaS features.

There are several benefits in using Terraform vs. cloud native services. You don't want to get locked in to a specific cloud; this is something many customers struggle with and something very important to consider when it comes to architecting a solution or leveraging native cloud services.

Terraform is a cloud-agnostic tool that helps plan, orchestrate, and deploy infrastructure to multiple clouds. You can even deploy an infrastructure that is comprised of multiple providers; for example, deploying a server in AWS and using Google Cloud for DNS and IP address assigned to the server.

Here are some key features that make it compelling.

- **Infrastructure as Code**. Infrastructure is described using a declarative syntax. Infrastructure can be shared and reused.

- **Execution plans**. Terraform's execution plan allows you to see what would happen should you choose to build the infrastructure by executing the `apply` command. It's a good sanity check before actually building the infrastructure.

- **Resource graph**. Terraform builds graphs of the resources being used and their dependencies.

- **Change automation**. Complex change-sets can be applied to infrastructure with minimal human intervention.

- **Versioned infrastructure**. Much like software, you can use Git, Bitbucket, or GitLab to version your infrastructure.

- **Reusable infrastructure modules**. Imagine empowering your developers to easily use the latest version of a SharePoint farm to deploy a test environment in minutes. Now you need to extend that farm capability to include other infrastructure capabilities; therefore, you create and publish your own modules for anyone to consume within your enterprise, or you open source said modules.

Let's look at an example configuration file (see Listing 1-1) that describes a web front-end server deployed to AWS.

Listing 1-1. Terraform Configuration File Example That Describes Web Front End Server to Be Deployed to AWS

```
provider "aws" {
  region = "${var.region}"
}

resource "aws_eip" "default" {
  instance = "${aws_instance.spfarm_WFE1.id}"
  vpc      = true
}
resource "aws_instance" "spfarm_WFE1" {

  instance_type = "${var.instance_type}"
  ami = "${lookup(var.amis, var.region)}"

  # the security group
  vpc_security_group_ids = ["${aws_security_group.sg_spfarm.id}"]
  key_name = "${aws_key_pair.spfarmkeypair.key_name}"

  # the main VPC
  subnet_id = "${aws_subnet.main-public-1.id}"

  tags {
    "Name" = "${var.sprole_name} - ${aws_security_group.sg_spfarm.id}",
    "Server Role" = "Web-Front End",
```

```
    "Tier" = "Presentation Layer",
    "Location" = "AWS Cloud",
    "Environment" = "Staging"
  }
```

You will notice that there are items that look like variables. Terraform allows us to define variables, and then uses interpolation as shown in the example code, to inject the values of these variables. This is very powerful because it allows us to create clean configuration files. It also allows a single place to change things globally, typically on a Terraform project where you have a `variables.tf` file, which includes global variables.

Idempotency

One common trait of DevOps tools is the ability to run a given task and only update items that need to be updated based on the instructions. Merriam-Webster defines *idempotent* as "relating to or being a mathematical quantity which when applied to itself under a given binary operation (such as multiplication) equals itself." For example, with Ansible, you may run a playbook against a group of machines in an inventory called Application Servers. One of the playbook's tasks enables several features and roles, including the Web Server (IIS) role. Now let's assume that one of those machines already has the Web Server (IIS) role enabled. Ansible checks for this and simply skips the task, and either outputs to a log or your terminal—a status indicating it skipped the machine because the role was already configured.

If we run that same playbook a second time, we will get the same message indicating that it skipped that specific machine for the same reason.

That is idempotency, and it is used in many tools, including Terraform and Ansible. This saves time, as you avoid performing tasks that are not necessary within your workflow.

Configuration Management

Practicing DevOps also involves dealing with configuration management in an elegant and efficient manner. Ansible stands out, as it has a growing community, is a leader in configuration management, and is quite capable of dealing with provisioning, app deployment, continuous delivery, security and compliance, and orchestration. As you can see, Ansible can do more than just configuration management, and in fact, there is an overlap in capabilities when combined with other tools. Ultimately, it is a matter of preference and what your organization feels comfortable investing in.

Note   In this book, we use Ansible primarily as a *configuration management* tool; clearly, that is just scratching the surface of its capabilities. Later in this book, we cover how to use Ansible Tower, which is a web-based solution that makes Ansible easier for IT teams to use. It's designed to be the hub for all of your automation tasks and a setup for enterprise-level environments.

Ansible is minimal by design, with a low learning curve; yet, its capabilities are highly powerful. It uses declarative YAML and JSON to describe playbooks, which themselves contain tasks that can be executed on target machines.

Ansible is an open source configuration management, deployment, and orchestration tool. Unlike many tools in this space, Ansible is *agentless*, meaning nothing is installed on the target servers to be managed. It can manage Linux and Windows machines, respectively. Windows machines are managed using WinRM, whereas Linux machines are managed using SSH.

The following are Ansible's key features.

- A consistent, repeatable, reliable approach automates and manages different environments, such as testing, staging, and production.

- It uses YAML, a human-readable and popular markup language used by other open source systems for declarative configuration.

- It is extensible via modules. There are about 750 community provided powerful modules for both Linux and Windows.

- It integrates well with other open source tools, such as Vagrant, Packer, and Terraform.

- Agentless, it integrates with identity management systems such as Active Directory and runs commands under user-supplied credentials. It does not require high privileges.

- It manages systems via authoring reusable, version-controlled playbooks and roles to manage a desired state.

Virtualization

Bringing agility to DevOps practices involves having the ability to stand up and tear down testing and staging environments at will—in minutes. Enter Vagrant. HashiCorp, the maker of Vagrant describes it as follows: "Vagrant is a tool for building and managing virtual machine environments in a single workflow. With an easy-to-use workflow and focus on automation, Vagrant lowers development environment setup time, increases production parity, and makes the 'works on my machine' excuse a relic of the past." (www.vagrantup.com)

Vagrant allows you to build environments in a repeatable, reliable fashion, and with a single workflow. Vagrant uses the provider concept to provision virtual machines for different platforms such as VirtualBox, VMWare, AWS, Azure, and Docker. Vagrant then uses provisioners such as Chef, Puppet, and Ansible to execute configuration management tasks.

Let's look at Vagrantfile shown in Listing 1-2, which contains an Ansible provider to configure a Windows Server 2016 VirtualBox machine as a domain controller. This is a Vagrantfile that we use later in this book to provision the testing environment SharePoint domain controller server, to run configuration management on that machine to promote it as a domain controller, and to create the SharePoint service accounts.

Note   Don't worry if you don't understand the details of this file. In subsequent chapters, we go over the details of this Vagrantfile to help you understand what exactly it is doing and how it all comes together when building the virtualized testing SharePoint farm environment.

Listing 1-2. Actual Vagrantfile Used to Bring up a SharePoint Farm and Configure Servers

```
require 'yaml'
require 'json'

error = Vagrant::Errors::VagrantError
machines = YAML.load_file 'vagrant-machines.yaml'
ANSIBLE_RAW_SSH_ARGS = []
```

```ruby
#delete the inventory file if it exists so we can recreate
File.delete("ansible/hosts_test_env.yaml")

File.open("ansible/hosts_test_env.yaml" ,'w') do |f|
  machines.each do |machine|
    f.write "#{machine[0]}:\n"
    f.write "     Hosts:\n"
    f.write "          #{machine[1]['name']}:\n"
    f.write "            ansible_ssh_host: #{machine[1]['ip_address']}\n"
  end
end

Vagrant.configure(2) do |config|

  config.vm.box_check_update = false

  machines.each do |machine|

    name = machine[1]['name']
    box =  machine[1]['box']
    role = machine[1]['role']
    hostname = machine[1]['hostname']

    providers = machine[1]['providers']
    memory = machine[1]['memory'] || '512'
    default = machine[1]['default'] || false
    ip_address = machine[1]['ip_address']

    # insert the private key from the host machine to the guest
    ANSIBLE_RAW_SSH_ARGS << "-o IdentityFile=~/.vagrant.d/insecure_private_
    key"

    fail error.new, 'machines must contain a name' if name.nil?

    config.vm.define name, primary: default, autostart: default do |cfg|
    cfg.vm.hostname = hostname
        # credentials
    cfg.winrm.username = "vagrant"
```

```
cfg.winrm.password = "vagrant"
cfg.vm.guest = :windows
cfg.vm.communicator = "winrm"
cfg.windows.halt_timeout = 35
config.vm.boot_timeout = 400

#configure the network for this machine
cfg.vm.network "private_network", ip: ip_address
cfg.vm.network :forwarded_port, guest: 5985, host: 5985, id: "winrm",
auto_correct: true
cfg.vm.network :forwarded_port, guest: 3389, host: 3389, id: "rdp",
auto_correct: true
cfg.vm.network :forwarded_port, guest: 22, host: 2222, id: "ssh",
auto_correct: true

  if box
    cfg.vm.box = box
  elsif box_url && box_name
    cfg.vm.box = box_name
    cfg.vm.box_url = box_url
  else
    fail error.new, 'machines must contain box or box_name and box_url'
  end

  if providers == 'virtualbox'
    cfg.vm.provider :virtualbox do |v|
      v.gui = true
      v.customize ["modifyvm", :id, "--memory", memory]
      v.customize ["modifyvm", :id, "--cpus", 2]
      v.customize ["modifyvm", :id, "--vram", 128]
      v.customize ["modifyvm", :id, "--clipboard", "bidirectional"]
      v.customize ["modifyvm", :id, "--accelerate3d", "on"]
      v.customize ["modifyvm", :id, "--accelerate2dvideo", "on"]
    end
  end
```

```
# we can insert provisioners here to inject additional scripts if
needed
# sample below.
#cfg.vm.provision "shell", path: "./ansible/roles/internal/common/
files/openssh.ps1"

# Use specific Ansible Playbooks and other provisioners based on SP
Machine Role
if role == 'DomainController'
  cfg.vm.provision :ansible do |ansible|
      #let's configure the domain controler and add
      # a) the SP Service Accounts
      # b) Sample User Accounts
      ansible.limit = "domaincontrollers"
      ansible.playbook = "ansible/plays/domaincontroller.yml"
      ansible.inventory_path = "ansible/test.ini"
      ansible.verbose = "vvvv"
      ansible.raw_ssh_args = ANSIBLE_RAW_SSH_ARGS
  end
elsif role == 'Front-End'
  # we must set the network interface DNS server accordingly
  # before we join the machine to the domain

  config.vm.provision "shell", path: "./ansible/roles/internal/
  domaincontroller/files/setDNS.ps1", args:"-DNS 192.1.68.2.19
  -Network 192.168.2.16"

  # join machine to domain name
  cfg.vm.provision :ansible do |ansible|
    ansible.limit = "webservers"
    ansible.playbook = "ansible/plays/webservers.yml"
    ansible.inventory_path = "ansible/test.ini"
    ansible.verbose = "vvvv"
    ansible.raw_ssh_args = ANSIBLE_RAW_SSH_ARGS
  end
end
```

```
      end
    end
  end
```

From a DevOps perspective, Vagrant provides a disposable environment and consistent workflow for developing and testing infrastructure management scripts such as PowerShell or Ansible modules.

Vagrant excels tremendously in enforcing environmental parity, which helps avoid surprises in the deployment of applications on top of the infrastructure.

Machine Imaging (Prebaked Images)

Machine imaging is a common practice in IT shops. However, until not too long ago, all the imaging had to be done manually, which led to errors and a costly and tedious process to create and update "blessed" images in the enterprise.

Introducing Packer

Packer is an open source tool for creating identical machines in multiple platforms, such as AWS, OpenStack, Azure, and VMWare. Packer runs on every major operating system and is very lightweight.

Today, when we talk about images, we think of them as a unit that contains preconfigured operating system and software packages. This unit is used to launch and destroy instances in seconds—much like Amazon EC2 instances, which are launched based on AMIs with preinstalled operating systems such as Linux, Red Hat, Windows 2012, Windows 10, and so forth.

These images can also be launched on VirtualBox, VMWare Fusion for Mac, and other virtualization platforms.

Tip   Later in this book, we use Packer to create a base Windows 2016 Server image for our SharePoint farm, which we then launch using Terraform.

Packer is a modern open source tool; however, it also embraces configuration management tools such as Puppet and Ansible to install and configure software packages. The possibilities are endless; you can make a demo of custom software, or in our case, showcase the latest SharePoint version, launched in seconds.

The following are the key features/advantages of Packer.

- **Ultra-fast infrastructure deployment**. Launches completely configured images to development, staging, and production environments within seconds.

- **Portability**. Because Packer creates identical images for multiple platforms, you can run a production environment in AWS, staging in Google Cloud, or a development VirtualBox environment locally on a laptop, for example. This is portability at its finest.

- **Stability**. Because software packages and configuration management takes place at the time of building the machine, problems are detected and fixed early, rather than finding issues when images are launched in different environments.

There are many great use cases for Packer. Because Packer is command-line driven, building it into the continuous delivery pipeline is possible. In this scenario, a service like Jenkins may run Packer commands to build the image, which itself contains Serverspec tests to run at build time. Should the test pass, new images are created for multiple platforms, and then launched and tested.

It is worth noting that the HashiCorp Atlas site (at the time of writing this book) is going through a transformation. HashiCorp now offers each product independently. In other words, if your organization uses Terraform Enterprise only, this is possible. In return, this allows a company to integrate the usage of the individual product into its own delivery pipeline as it sees fit, rather than using the stack of the HashiCorp products (what used to be Atlas) in one workflow.

Benefits of DevOps Practices

We've covered the practices and values of DevOps, and you learned which open source tools are at the core of the preferred toolchain. However, you want to know the benefits of practicing DevOps within the enterprise. DevOps teams increased from 16% in 2014, to 19% in 2015, to 22% in 2016, and to 27% in 2017.[1]

---

[1]2017 State of DevOps Report: New findings on transformational leadership, automation practices and more, Puppet, `https://puppet.com/resources/whitepaper/state-of-devops-report?pcnav=off&pctiles=off&ls=Campaigns&lsd=Search&cid=7010f000001eVgM&utm_medium=paid-search&utm_campaign=Q2FY18_AMER_All_CAMPGN_SER_BING_2017-DO-rpt&utm_source=bing&utm_content=2017-devops-report&utm_term=devops`

The DevOps movement continues to gain momentum as mentioned in the *State of DevOps Report*, published by Puppet and DORA, a DevOps research and assessment organization. You might wonder if this is applicable or helpful to an IT professional working on the Microsoft stack of technologies. And the answer is yes; in fact, given Microsoft's recent open source track record and initiatives, there is a lot of toolchain modernization within this ecosystem; it will only become far more relevant in the near future. As an IT pro, it is beneficial to become acquainted with the DevOps practices and apply them to your work to enhance your skills and further your career.

With Microsoft's "love" for Linux, it is gradually becoming easier to use Microsoft's own tools on systems other than Windows. One example is .NET Core now being open sourced and capable of running on Linux. Another example is the ability to run SQL Server on Linux.

Why DevOps Practices Matter When It Comes to SharePoint

So how does DevOps relate or is relevant to the SharePoint platform and related technologies, such as Azure, AWS, and other clouds where one can deploy it?

Having been around in the SharePoint consulting world for over 17 years, we've seen a fair number IT shops manually build virtual machines for a SharePoint farm more often than I'd like to admit. This ultimately causes a lot of grief for IT pros, the business stakeholders, and the end client due to inconsistency and an error-prone approach. Not to mention, the time it takes to build out a farm manually.

Clearly, the open source tools that we've discussed have not been around for that long. But now that they have been around for a few years, shouldn't we feel the urgency to automate not only the installation of SharePoint but also the provisioning of virtualized environments across clouds and on-premises?

Note   Many SharePoint administrators are already aware that PowerShell automation exists for a good portion of the steps needed to install SharePoint. In this book, we look beyond that and cover automated installation, configuration management, and provisioning of the entire virtualized farm on-premises or in the cloud.

Enterprise environments can no longer afford to work with arcane methodologies if they are to be successful in delivering products and services to both internal and external customers.

Multiple surveys and research documents published by companies like Puppet, Amazon, and Ansible all convey the same message: DevOps practices lead to higher IT performance, which, in return, delivers improved business outcomes as measured by productivity, profitability, and market share.

DevOps benefits span far beyond financial ramifications, as organizations are now capable of achieving their vision and goals irrespective of what that vision is. In other words, DevOps is quite relevant, no matter the business a company is in.

Given these findings, it is paramount to have engaged leadership to ensure success in adopting DevOps practices, because these are the people that have the ability to make decisions and the budget, and who are able to provide support in the midst of a transformation.

Applying DevOps Practices

Now that you are aware of some of the benefits of DevOps, let's look at some areas where applying DevOps practices and using open source tools may prove to be extremely beneficial in the SharePoint realm.

Use Infrastructure as Code to Provision SharePoint Dev and Test Environments

As mentioned earlier on this chapter, the operations team also treats everything as code and leverages versioning when applying DevOps practices in addition to automation as one of the core values of DevOps. How then can we avoid manually provisioning servers that form part of a SharePoint Farm? We use **Infrastructure as Code** (IaC). The same code can be used to provision staging, testing and production environments to multiple target environments such as Azure, AWS or on-premises.

When a new developer joins an organization, it now takes a matter of minutes to provision a local environment by using previously created code that describes the infrastructure for a local environment. In this scenario, the developer can use the Vagrantfile previously developed by the ops team (which is most likely in source control such as GitHub) to quickly provision any environment with a simple command such as vagrant up.

This effectively streamlines the infrastructure and provisioning of identical environments for staging, testing, and production, which eliminates any surprises that may affect timelines.

Continuous Integration/Continuous Deployment

You might recall that DevOps practices include automated testing and CI/CD. How can we apply automation now that we have our Vagrantfile?

Before the development team can provision their own environment, the operations team might code the Vagrantfile, and add configuration management and test scripts to ensure that the environments being provisioned are successful. To do this, they can add actual test scripts and run automated testing using Jenkins, for example. If the tests pass, the Vagrantfile is versioned and stored in GitHub, which makes the latest version available to other teams in the organization. Anytime a developer needs to spin up a development environment that mirrors production, he/she simply gets the latest Vagrantfile from GitHub, and has an environment in minutes. This process was shown in Figure 1-3.

Configuration Management

Another major component of DevOps is configuration management. Tools like Ansible help automate the provisioning of various software packages; for example, an Ansible playbook that contains various standard tasks to perform machine updates, or install Git, Chocolatey, and other packages on virtual machines. All of this can happen when you initially spin up the machine using Vagrant or make updates to existing machines.

In another scenario, a systems administrator executes ad hoc Ansible commands against a group of machines (like all WFEs in the SharePoint farm) to install a SharePoint hotfix or patch.

It is easy to see the power of automation vs. manually remoting into each machine, installing packages, and restarting the machine, all of which may lead to missing steps, errors, and a lot of dedicated time to execute.

As you've learned in this chapter, Ansible's capabilities span far more than just configuration management. This book's exercises, however, focus on the core capability to manage a SharePoint farm.

Summary

In this chapter, you learned about DevOps practices and values, why DevOps is an important practice to adopt in any organization, and the tools that enable you to practice DevOps when deploying identical environments and managing a SharePoint farm in an enterprise environment.

In the next chapter, we walk you through the setup of all the tools that you need to follow the exercises in this book.

CHAPTER 2

Getting up and Running: Set up Your Environment

Now that you understand what DevOps is all about, let's prepare our environment to follow the exercises in this book. Having your environment configured properly is paramount to being able to execute the exercises. The following will help you configure the proper tooling and settings to enable the successful creation of your SharePoint deployment and configuration.

This chapter walks you through the initial setup of the various open source tools that you need to follow the various exercises in subsequent chapters.

Note Because Ansible does not support Windows as a host, we will only focus on OS X and Linux as our host platforms. If you are using Windows, installing a VM with a Linux OS will allow you to perform the following setup.

Our Environment

All the sample code, terminal commands, and usage of these tools are executed on a MacBook Pro (OS X Sierra 10.12.5). All of these tools are available on the latest versions of OS X and most Linux distributions. As such, we will only focus on these operating systems in the exercises.

© Oscar Medina, Ethan Schumann 2018

O. Medina and E. Schumann, *DevOps for SharePoint*, https://doi.org/10.1007/978-1-4842-3688-8_2

Our Project Workflow

The exercises in this book follow a workflow. There is a sequence to how we want to implement things; therefore, we recommend that you follow the chapter sequence. The following are the workflow steps.

1. Build a generic Packer Windows image.

2. Build a Vagrant test environment SharePoint Farm.

3. Build production images using Packer (AWS and Azure).

4. Deploy an infrastructure using Terraform (AWS and Azure).

As you can see in Figure 2-1, Packer is used. We use Packer later in this book to create a "golden image" for our SharePoint farm.

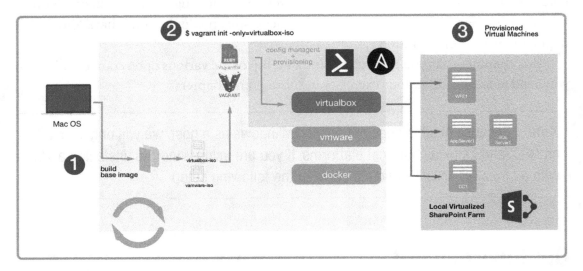

Figure 2-1. *Mac OS X Ansible control machine responsible for building a SharePoint Vagrant environment*

Figure 2-1 depicts the environment used for the exercises in this book. It shows a laptop with Vagrant to build boxes for the VirtualBox provider, and it uses both PowerShell and Ansible for configuration management.

The following software packages are used throughout the book's exercises:

- Git

- Vagrant

- Packer

- Ansible

- Terraform

The following section walks you through the installation of these packages.

Tip   Any source code or other supplementary material referenced by the authors in this book is available to readers on GitHub via the book's product page, located at `www.apress.com/ISBN13`. For more information, please visit `www.apress.com/source-code`. You may choose to clone the repository and follow the exercises in this book. See the "About the GitHub Repository" section later in this chapter.

Install an Open Source Toolchain

All subsequent chapters on this book make use of several tools. This section guides you through installing the prerequisite toolchain needed for the book's exercises.

Install Git

For Windows, you can install a PowerShell native tool called posh-git. This ships with all the standard functionality of Git and is usable inside of a standard PowerShell terminal. Note that you should have PowerShell 5.x installed.

Install posh-git Using Chocolatey on Windows

As an administrator, run the following.

```
C:\choco install poshgit
```

Install Terraform

Terraform can be installed in several ways, such as downloading the binaries directly from the HashiCorp site at `www.terraform.io/downloads.html`. There are several other options as outlined next.

Install Using Homebrew on Mac OS X

The first method is to install it using Homebrew on OS X by executing the following command.

```
$ brew install terraform
```

Later, when a new version is out, we can easily update it by executing the following command.

```
$ brew upgrade terraform
```

Verifying Installation

To verify that all is working properly, you can issue the following command.

```
$ terraform -v
```

The output of this should be Terraform v0.9.x, for example, or whatever version is installed.

Install Using Terraform Version Manager

Although it is not required to complete the exercises in this book, Terraform Version Manager is very handy when working with large environments. This is due to the rapid release and deprecation of Terraform features as the tool continues to evolve. You can also use tfenv, an open source tool that is available at `https://github.com/kamatama41/tfenv`. It works on OS X, Linux, and Windows.

tfenv allows you to manage multiple installed versions of Terraform. You can install it by executing the following command.

```
$ brew install tfenv
```

Install Using Other Methods

There are several configuration management tools that allow you to install and use Terraform.

- A Puppet Module for Terraform (`https://forge.puppet.com/inkblot/terraform`)

- Docker Container with Terraform (`https://hub.docker.com/r/hashicorp/terraform`)

- Ansible Role for Terraform (`https://galaxy.ansible.com/azavea/terraform`)

Install Packer

The most common installation method is to download the binaries; however, there are a couple of alternative methods that we cover here.

Install Using Homebrew on Mac OS X

To install Packer, execute the following command.

```
$ brew install packer
```

Verifying Installation

To verify that Packer is installed correctly, issue the following command.

```
$ packer -v
```

This should output the version installed.

Install Vagrant

Vagrant can be installed in several ways, including downloading the binaries from the HashiCorp site at `www.vagrantup.com/downloads.html`.

Install Using Homebrew on Mac OS X

In addition to Brew, you want to make sure that you have Homebrew-Cask, which extends Homebrew. It is available via, Brew of course!

What is Homebrew-Cask? Its authors describe it as follows: "Homebrew-Cask extends Homebrew and brings its elegance, simplicity, and speed to macOS applications and large binaries alike. It only takes 1 line in your shell to reach 3652 Casks maintained by 4612 contributors." (`www.caskroom.github.io`)

To install Homebrew-Cask, simply execute the following command.

```
$ brew tap caskroom/cask
```

Verify that installation was successful by executing `brew cask` on your terminal. You should see output that looks like the following code.

```
$ brew cask
brew-cask provides a friendly homebrew-style CLI workflow for the
administration of macOS applications distributed as binaries.

Commands:
    --version             displays the Homebrew-Cask version
    audit                 verifies installability of Casks
    cat                   dump raw source of the given Cask to the
                          standard output
    cleanup               cleans up cached downloads and tracker symlinks
    create                creates the given Cask and opens it in an editor
    doctor                checks for configuration issues
    edit                  edits the given Cask
    fetch                 downloads remote application files to local
                          cache
    home                  opens the homepage of the given Cask
    info                  displays information about the given Cask
    install               installs the given Cask
    list                  with no args, lists installed Casks; given
                          installed Casks, lists staged files
    outdated              list the outdated installed Casks
    reinstall             reinstalls the given Cask
```

```
search                  searches all known Casks
style                   checks Cask style using RuboCop
uninstall               uninstalls the given Cask
zap                     zaps all files associated with the given Cask
```

See also "man brew-cask"

Now that you have Homebrew-Cask, let's install Vagrant. Execute the following command.

```
$ brew cask install vagrant
```

Verifying Installation

To verify that Vagrant is installed correctly, issue the following command.

```
$ vagrant -v
```

This should output the version installed.

Install Ansible

Now let's install the configuration management tool that we will use throughout our exercises. If you've installed the other tools using Homebrew, then this first option should be the easiest for you. Also, be sure that you have Python 2.x installed because it is a prerequisite.

Note   Windows machines are not supported control machines for Ansible; therefore, you want to use a Vagrant box with Linux for this purpose. The following section explains an Ansible provided Vagrant box to quickly get up and running with Ansible.

Install Using Homebrew on Mac OS X

```
$ brew install ansible
```

Verify installation by executing the following command with the output shown, depending on the version that you installed. In our case, it was Ansible 2.3.1.0. The output also shows that we are running Python 2.7.13. Note that Ansible and Python are frequently updated, so you will most likely have a newer version.

```
$ ansible --version
ansible 2.3.1.0
  config file =
  configured module search path = Default w/o overrides
  python version = 2.7.13 (default, Apr  4 2017, 08:47:57) [GCC 4.2.1
Compatible Apple LLVM 8.1.0 (clang-802.0.38)]
```

Install Using PIP (Python Package Manager) on Mac OS X

According to the Ansible documentation, this is the preferred installation. In our experience, however, using Homebrew works just as well. Install by executing the following command.

```
$ sudo pip install ansible
```

You can verify installation by simply executing the following command, which should output the version of Ansible installed.

```
$ ansible --version
```

Use an Ansible-Provided Vagrant Machine as a Control Machine

You can opt to use the Ansible Vagrant machine to quickly get up and running.

This machine contains Ansible Tower, a powerful software package that allows you to centralize all of your Ansible playbooks and deployments. Some key features include role-based access control, job scheduling, and a nice visual representation of your inventory.

Tip   Although we do not use Ansible Tower, we highly recommend using it as part of your enterprise level DevOps tool-chain given the added features such as access control, job scheduling, dashboards and workflow control.

Execute the following commands.

1. `$ mkdir ansibletower`

2. `$ cd ansibletower`

3. `$ vagrant init ansible/tower`

4. $ vagrant up -provider virtualbox

5. $ vagrant ssh

Executing the command in item 5 outputs the username and password that you need to access the Ansible Tower web-based interface.

```
$ vagrant ssh
Last login: Sat Jul  8 02:34:10 2017 from gateway

  Welcome to Ansible Tower!

  Log into the web interface here:

    https://10.42.0.42/

    Username: admin
    Password: NA7nr4JuvLDT

  The documentation for Ansible Tower is available here:

    http://www.ansible.com/tower/

  For help, visit  http://support.ansible.com/
[vagrant@ansible-tower ~]$
```

Since you are now SSHed into the box, you can easily execute Ansible commands. For example, to get the Ansible version used on the Vagrant machine, execute the following command, and you will see similar output.

```
[vagrant@ansible-tower ~]$ ansible --version
ansible 2.3.0.0
  config file = /etc/ansible/ansible.cfg
  configured module search path = Default w/o overrides
  python version = 2.7.5 (default, Nov  6 2016, 00:28:07) [GCC 4.8.5
  20150623 (Red Hat 4.8.5-11)]
[vagrant@ansible-tower ~]$
```

Once configured, you are ready to follow along.

About the GitHub Repository

The entire GitHub repository for the exercises in this book is available on the GitHub website. You may use this repository as a starting point, or you may create a blank project and incorporate some of the components. It really is up to you. Just know that we are referencing this specific structure and repository while working through the various exercises.

Tip   To set up Git, please see `https://help.github.com/articles/set-up-git`. This covers initial setup, including SSH keys for authentication.

Getting Started

The first thing that you want to do is clone the repository. This allows you to run the project locally and modify it as you see fit. To do that, simply execute the following command in your terminal.

```
$ git clone git@github.com:SharePointOscar/vagrant-ansible-packer-spfarm.git
```

Once you've cloned the repository, you are ready to follow our first exercise in Chapter 3.

Summary

In this chapter, we installed all the open source tools needed to execute the exercises in this book. In the next chapter, we start our first exercise and build a test environment for our SharePoint farm using Vagrant and Ansible. This serves as a great starting point, which we will build on to create the proper artifact using Packer and to deploy to Azure and AWS.

CHAPTER 3

Build a Dev SharePoint Farm with Vagrant and ServerSpec

In the previous chapter, we walked through the required setup of our toolchain and cloning the GitHub repository for this book. With all this in place, we are ready to start with the first step in our overall workflow.

This chapter walks you through creating a test environment using Vagrant and testing it using the ServerSpec framework. We perform tests because we want to make sure that any configuration management tasks we execute have successfully executed and that the software is configured per our requirements.

The overall solution, which is intended to run locally on a developer's machine, looks like the diagram shown in Figure 3-1.

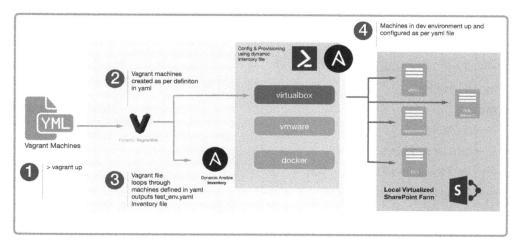

Figure 3-1. *Vagrant machines. YAML is responsible for defining the Ansible inventory file.*

© Oscar Medina, Ethan Schumann 2018
O. Medina and E. Schumann, *DevOps for SharePoint*, https://doi.org/10.1007/978-1-4842-3688-8_3

GitHub Repository Project Structure

The GitHub repository is structured with subprojects to separate things by tool and area, such as Infrastructure as Code (Terraform), configuration management (Ansible), and image baking (Packer). For example, all Ansible-related things are under the Ansible folder. All Terraform (Infrastructure as Code) assets are located under the Terraform folder. The Packer-related templates are within its folder. Listing 3-1 is a view of the project structure.

Listing 3-1. GitHub Repository Project Structure

```
$ tree -L 2
.
├── HOWTOUSE.md
├── LICENSE
├── README.md
├── Vagrantfile
├── ansible
│   ├── development.ini
│   ├── extensions
│   ├── group_vars
│   ├── hosts_test_env.yaml
│   ├── plays
│   ├── production.ini
│   ├── roles
│   ├── test.ini
│   └── test_env.yaml
├── ansible.cfg
├── packer
│   ├── README.MD
│   ├── answer_files
│   ├── atlas-aws-win2016.json
│   ├── aws-scripts
│   ├── aws-win2016.json
│   ├── floppy
│   ├── packer_cache
```

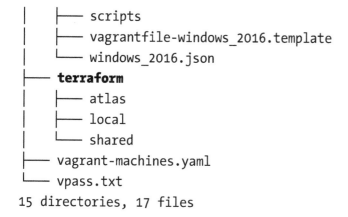

```
|       ├── scripts
|       ├── vagrantfile-windows_2016.template
|       └── windows_2016.json
├── terraform
|       ├── atlas
|       ├── local
|       └── shared
├── vagrant-machines.yaml
└── vpass.txt
15 directories, 17 files
```

The Vagrant aspect of this project is comprised of two files: `vagrant-machines.yaml` and the Vagrantfile.

We will work with these two files to build our SharePoint farm. But before we do that, we need to create our "golden image," which is considered the base image with preloaded software packages, updates, and so forth.

Tip   For this initial step in the workflow, we create a basic Windows Server 2016 image, but it is not the final image because we are testing our configuration management scripts while building the Vagrant SharePoint test environment. Think of it as an iterative process.

Creating a Windows-Based Image Using Packer

Our first step in the overall workflow is to create a "golden image" with the provisioned software packages, which serves as the basis for building out our SharePoint farm using Vagrant. To do this, we've made use of an open source repository from Stefan Scherer, from which we've extracted some content, modified it, and then integrated it into our repo for convenience. Specifically, we added the `shutdown` command to ensure a Sysprep since we are building a domain controller, and we don't want any duplicate SID error messages.

You can find the packer folder within our GitHub repository. Let's go over the contents of the packer folder within the repo and highlight a few things as it relates to creating our image.

Disabling Windows Updates

For the purpose of this walkthrough, we want to ensure that when we build our image, the updates do not get downloaded and installed, because it is a very time-consuming process. Therefore, we need to first modify the XML file under the answer_files directory, and then open the file at 2016/Autounattend.xml and uncomment, as showing in Listing 3-2.

Listing 3-2. Ensure the Answer File Has This Section Uncommented

```
<!-- WITHOUT WINDOWS UPDATES -->

 <SynchronousCommand wcm:action="add">
    <CommandLine>cmd.exe /c
    C:\Windows\System32\WindowsPowerShell\v1.0\powershell.exe -File
    a:\enable-winrm.ps1</CommandLine>
    <Description>Enable WinRM</Description>
    <Order>99</Order>
 </SynchronousCommand>

<!-- END WITHOUT WINDOWS UPDATES -->
```

Tip   You can follow detailed instructions on updates in the README.md file within the repository.

The Packer Template

Our Packer template uses Windows Server 2016, which is a supported OS for SharePoint 2016. The file that we will edit and modify is named windows_2016.json. It is a template that Packer uses to build the image.

Tip   Packer templates are extremely helpful because you can easily push them to source control and use the typical pull request method to review changes prior to building the next version. We highly recommend versioning your Packer templates as part of your workflow.

Packer builders allow us to build images for different virtualization providers, such as VMWare, VirtualBox, Hyper-V, Docker, and AWS, to name a few. We look at the VirtualBox builder through this exercise. The following is a snippet of what this template looks like.

```
{
  "builders": [
    ….
    {
      "type": "virtualbox-iso",
      "communicator": "winrm",
      "iso_url": "{{user `iso_url`}}",
      "iso_checksum_type": "{{user `iso_checksum_type`}}",
      "iso_checksum": "{{user `iso_checksum`}}",
      "headless": true,
      "boot_wait": "2m",
      "winrm_username": "vagrant",
      "winrm_password": "vagrant",
      "winrm_timeout": "6h",
      "shutdown_command": "A:/shutdown-Packer.bat",
      "guest_os_type": "Windows2012_64",
      "guest_additions_mode": "disable",
      "disk_size": 61440,
      "floppy_files": [
        "{{user `autounattend`}}",
        "./scripts/unattend.xml",
        "./scripts/shutdown-Packer.bat",
        "./floppy/WindowsPowershell.lnk",
        "./floppy/PinTo10.exe",
        "./scripts/disable-screensaver.ps1",
        "./scripts/disable-winrm.ps1",
        "./scripts/enable-winrm.ps1",
        "./scripts/microsoft-updates.bat",
        "./scripts/win-updates.ps1",
        "./scripts/oracle-cert.cer"
      ],
```

```
    "vboxmanage": [
      [
        "modifyvm",
        "{{.Name}}",
        "--memory",
        "2048"
      ],
      [
        "modifyvm",
        "{{.Name}}",
        "--cpus",
        "2"
      ]
    ]
  }
],
"provisioners": [
  {
    "type": "windows-shell",
    "execute_command": "{{ .Vars }} cmd /c \"{{ .Path }}\"",
    "scripts": [
      "./scripts/vm-guest-tools.bat",
      "./scripts/enable-rdp.bat"
    ]
  },
  {
    "type": "powershell",
    "scripts": [
      "./scripts/debloat-windows.ps1"
    ]
  },
  {
    "type": "windows-restart"
  },
```

```
    {
      "type": "windows-shell",
      "execute_command": "{{ .Vars }} cmd /c \"{{ .Path }}\"",
      "scripts": [
        "./scripts/pin-powershell.bat",
        "./scripts/set-winrm-automatic.bat",
        "./scripts/compile-dotnet-assemblies.bat",
        "./scripts/uac-enable.bat",
        "./scripts/compact.bat"
      ]
    }
  ],
  "post-processors": [
    {
      "type": "vagrant",
      "keep_input_artifact": false,
      "output": "spfarm_base_windows_2016_{{.Provider}}.box",
      "vagrantfile_template": "vagrantfile-windows_2016.template"
    }
  ],
  "variables": {
    "iso_url": "http://care.dlservice.microsoft.com/dl/
    download/1/4/9/149D5452-9B29-4274-B6B3-5361DBDA30
    BC/14393.0.161119-1705.RS1_REFRESH_SERVER_EVAL_X64FRE_EN-US.ISO",
    "iso_checksum_type": "md5",
    "iso_checksum": "70721288BBCDFE3239D8F8C0FAE55F1F",
    "autounattend": "./answer_files/2016/Autounattend.xml",
    "hyperv_switchname": "{{env `hyperv_switchname`}}"
  }
}
```

Let's go over the sections of this template to fully understand what is needed and what we may change.

Builders

Builders are responsible for building and targeting images for the various platforms. Packer has several, including for VMWare, VirtualBox, EC2, and Docker. It is important to know that each builder has its own specifics when it comes to configuration.

Our Packer template contains metadata for floppy drives, which we populate with specific files that we need to be accessible as we build our image. Of special interest is "./scripts/shutdown-Packer.bat", which we use to ensure that Sysprep runs the first time that the machine boots.

In addition, the metadata includes "shutdown_command": "A:/shutdown-Packer.bat", which uses the file attached to the floppy drive.

Provisioners

Packer uses *provisioners* to install and configure software packages, patch the kernel, create domain users, and perform many actions at build time. There are several provisioners, including Ansible, PowerShell, Chef, Puppet, Salt, and Shell.

Tip   We use the Ansible provisioner to implement a lot of the configuration management when building a SharePoint farm.

Provisioners are executed in the order they appear on the template. For this template, we have several that further configure the image, including enabling RDP.

You can create a custom provisioner if need be. Packer is extensible via its plug-in mechanism.

Post Processors

Post processors run after the builders and provisioners. They are optional and can be used, for example, when uploading a box to the HashiCorp Vagrant cloud. Our template outputs a file with the .box extension. We use this file to add to the Vagrant list of boxes for later use.

Variables

Variables help you update your template in one place. The overall structure allows you to have a variables node with respective metadata. It is a best practice to always use variables and their values within the template because it makes updating so much easier.

Building the Box File

Now that our template is modified with all the metadata we need, we are ready to build a base Windows 2016 Server image for our SharePoint farm.

Within the /packer directory of the GitHub repository, execute the following command.

```
packer build --only=virtualbox-iso windows_2016.json
```

> **Note**   Please note that the resulting file can be fairly large, usually around 10GB, so be sure that you have plenty of disk space prior to running this command.

This process takes a while. You will see the virtual machine reboot as per the instructions in the "Provisioners" section in this chapter. Once it has completed, we have a .box file, which we now need to import into Vagrant. We do this by executing the following command from the root of the GitHub project directory.

```
vagrant box add sharepointoscar/spfarm_base_windows2016 spfarm_base_
windows_2016_virtualbox.box
```

> **Tip**   The base box can be hosted on the Vagrant cloud or be internally accessible via a URL. Just know that the size of this artifact is around 4GB, so be sure that you have enough space.

We now have a base image that we can use for our Vagrant environment. Once this task is completed, we can switch over to our other GitHub repository for this project.

Building the Vagrant SharePoint Test Environment

Now that we've gone through the Packer build process, we have a base box that Vagrant can use, which we specify in our Vagrantfile as the base box to use for our SharePoint farm.

We need to configure our boxes based on the SharePoint role. To do this, we need to modify our Vagrantfile. However, recall that our solution has two files that need to be modified. This is because our Vagrant environment is a multibox environment, and we've implemented a flexible way to add or remove servers from the farm at build time.

Using SPAutoInstaller

We use Ansible to carry out specific tasks; however, SPAutoInstaller is incorporated because it is a comprehensive open source utility created by Brian Lalancette from Microsoft. You can find it at `http://spautoinstaller.com`. We use it to fully configure a SharePoint 2016 farm. Ansible helps us glue all the tasks together, as well as perform other configuration management tasks prior to installing SharePoint. Later in this chapter, we go over the specific Ansible task that triggers the SPAutoInstaller PowerShell scripts based on the SharePoint role that we are configuring using Ansible playbooks.

A Look at the Vagrant Multimachine Environment

Our solution uses two files to build the SharePoint farm: `vagrant-machines.yaml` and Vagrantfile. The YAML file is used to add or remove machines to the farm, and to specify various properties, including the farm role and IP address. The following are the full contents of the working file.

```
DomainControllers:
  name: DomainController1
  box: sharepointoscar/spfarm_base_windows2016
  hostname: SP2012R2AD
  role: DomainController
  memory: 2048
  default: true
  ip_address: 192.168.2.19
  providers: virtualbox

Webservers:
  name: WFE1
  box: sharepointoscar/spfarm_base_windows2016
  hostname: sp2016WFE
  role: Front-End
  memory: 2048
  default: false
  ip_address: 192.168.2.16
  providers: virtualbox
```

```
Databases:
  name: Database1
  box: sharepointoscar/spfarm_base_windows2016
  hostname: sp2016Sqlserver
  role: Database
  default: false
  ip_address: 192.168.2.17
  providers: virtualbox

AppServers:
  name: AppServer1
  box: sharepointoscar/spfarm_base_windows2016
  hostname: sp2016AppServer
  role: Application
  default: false
  ip_address: 192.168.2.18
  providers: virtualbox
```

Tip   The hostname metadata of each box must be unique, as is the case with the IP address.

We have grouped the boxes in their specific farm role, such as app servers, web servers, and so forth. With this in place, we can easily scale our farm and add an additional web server for instance. Then, the next time we provision our environment, Vagrant will spin up the new box.

A Closer Look at the Vagrantfile

The following is the full contents of the Vagrantfile. We will go through major sections of it below.

```
# -*- mode: ruby -*-
# vi: set ft=ruby :
  # TOPOLOGY - this topology is for a Small Non-High Availability MinRole
  Farm comprised of two servers plus
```

```ruby
# Domain Controller, Database Server and:
# a) WFE / Distributed Cache
# b) Application with Search Server
# for more details on SharePoint Topologies https://technet.microsoft.
com/en-us/library/mt743704(v=office.16).aspx
# also, be sure to take a look at the HOWTOUSE.md on this repository.

require 'yaml'
require 'json'

error = Vagrant::Errors::VagrantError
machines = YAML.load_file 'vagrant-machines.yaml'
ANSIBLE_RAW_SSH_ARGS = []

#delete the inventory file if it exists so we can recreate
File.delete("ansible/hosts_test_env.yaml")

File.open("ansible/hosts_test_env.yaml" ,'w') do |f|
  machines.each do |machine|
    f.write "#{machine[0]}:\n"
    f.write "    Hosts:\n"
    f.write "        #{machine[1]['name']}:\n"
    f.write "            ansible_ssh_host: #{machine[1]['ip_address']}\n"
  end
end

Vagrant.configure(2) do |config|

  config.vm.box_check_update = false

  machines.each do |machine|

    name = machine[1]['name']
    box =  machine[1]['box']
    role = machine[1]['role']
    hostname = machine[1]['hostname']

    providers = machine[1]['providers']
    memory = machine[1]['memory'] || '512'
    default = machine[1]['default'] || false
    ip_address = machine[1]['ip_address']
```

```
# insert the private key from the host machine to the guest
ANSIBLE_RAW_SSH_ARGS << "-o IdentityFile=~/.vagrant.d/insecure_private_key"

fail error.new, 'machines must contain a name' if name.nil?

config.vm.define name, primary: default, autostart: default do |cfg|
cfg.vm.hostname = hostname
    # credentials
cfg.winrm.username = "vagrant"
cfg.winrm.password = "vagrant"
cfg.vm.guest = :windows
cfg.vm.communicator = "winrm"
cfg.windows.halt_timeout = 35
cfg.vm.boot_timeout = 600

#configure the network for this machine
cfg.vm.network "private_network", ip: ip_address
cfg.vm.network :forwarded_port, guest: 5985, host: 5985, id: "winrm",
auto_correct: true
cfg.vm.network :forwarded_port, guest: 3389, host: 3389, id: "rdp",
auto_correct: true
cfg.vm.network :forwarded_port, guest: 22, host: 2222, id: "ssh",
auto_correct: true

cfg.vm.network :public_network
  if box
    cfg.vm.box = box
  elsif box_url && box_name
    cfg.vm.box = box_name
    cfg.vm.box_url = box_url
  else
    fail error.new, 'machines must contain box or box_name and box_url'
  end

  if providers == 'virtualbox'
    cfg.vm.provider :virtualbox do |v|
      v.gui = true
      v.customize ["modifyvm", :id, "--memory", memory]
      v.customize ["modifyvm", :id, "--cpus", 2]
```

```
      v.customize ["modifyvm", :id, "--vram", 128]
      v.customize ["modifyvm", :id, "--clipboard", "bidirectional"]
      v.customize ["modifyvm", :id, "--accelerate3d", "on"]
      v.customize ["modifyvm", :id, "--accelerate2dvideo", "on"]
    end
  end

  # we can insert provisioners here to inject additional scripts if
  needed
  # sample below.
  #cfg.vm.provision "shell", path: "./ansible/roles/internal/common/
  files/openssh.ps1"

  # Use specific Ansible Playbooks and other provisioners based on SP
  Machine Role
  if role == 'DomainController'
    cfg.vm.provision :ansible do |ansible|
        #let's configure the domain controler and add
        # a) the SP Service Accounts
        # b) Sample User Accounts
        ansible.limit = "domaincontrollers"
        ansible.playbook = "ansible/plays/domaincontroller.yml"
        ansible.inventory_path = "ansible/test.ini"
        ansible.verbose = "vvvv"
        ansible.raw_ssh_args = ANSIBLE_RAW_SSH_ARGS
    end
  elsif role == 'Front-End'
    # we must set the network interface DNS server accordingly
    # before we join the machien to the domain
    config.vm.provision "shell", path: "./ansible/roles/internal/
    domaincontroller/files/setDNS.ps1", args:"-DNS 192.1.68.2.19
    -Network 192.168.2.16"

    # join machine to domain name
    cfg.vm.provision :ansible do |ansible|
      ansible.limit = "webservers"
      ansible.playbook = "ansible/plays/webservers.yml"
      ansible.inventory_path = "ansible/test.ini"
```

```
      ansible.verbose = "vvvv"
      ansible.raw_ssh_args = ANSIBLE_RAW_SSH_ARGS
    end
  end
 end
end
end
```

This is a lot to take in, so let's go over some of the key elements in this file.

Building the Ansible Inventory Dynamically

Because we use Ansible as our provisioning tool, we must create an "inventory" file that keeps track of all the machines that Ansible should be able to reach and manage. These machines are grouped by the SharePoint role in our scenario. As you can imagine, things can get very complicated if we were to maintain the inventory file and the Vagrantfile manually, as it would effectively be more work to keep those two files in sync, as they should be. In other words, you never want to be in a situation where your Vagrantfile specifies a machine that does not exist in the Ansible inventory file and vice versa (see Figure 3-1).

In lines 21 to 36, the Vagrantfile deletes the previous file within the file system, and then creates a `File` object to write the new values based on the `vagrant-machines.yaml` definition. The new inventory file is then written to `ansible/hosts_test_env.yaml`, which is used both when provisioning using Vagrant and when executing ad hoc Ansible commands to run playbooks.

For each machine defined, it creates said machine, based on the base box and with specific virtualization provider, which in our case is VirtualBox. It ensures that the WinRM username and password are specified for Ansible to access for provisioning and configuration management tasks, which happens when the environment is brought up. This is because Vagrant has provisioners, and in our case, we use Ansible as a provisioner.

We then configure the network and ports. SSH, RDP, and WinRM are key to our configuration. We need to configure SSH so that Vagrant is able to access the machine. RDP is opened so that we can remote into the machine. WinRM is needed later to perform configuration management using Ansible.

Performing Ansible Provisioning Tasks Based on SharePoint Role

Our Vagrantfile language is Ruby; therefore, we can take advantage of all the Ruby goodness, which includes core conditional statements. For our Vagrant environment,

45

we want to ensure that only certain provisioning tasks or Ansible playbooks are executed based on the server SharePoint role.

The first role we handle is the domain controller, which is set up from scratch using Ansible and PowerShell. Once the domain controller is available, we bring up the rest of the machines in the farm and join them to the domain.

Because we use the Ansible provisioner within our Vagrantfile, Listing 3-3 is what the output looks like when we execute the command to bring up the domain controller role.

Listing 3-3. Ansible Provisioner Output When Bringing up the Domaincontroller1 Machine

```
PYTHONUNBUFFERED=1 ANSIBLE_FORCE_COLOR=true ANSIBLE_HOST_KEY_
CHECKING=false ANSIBLE_SSH_ARGS='-o UserKnownHostsFile=/dev/null -o
IdentitiesOnly=yes -i '/Users/sharepointoscar/.vagrant.d/insecure_
private_key' -o IdentityFile=~/.vagrant.d/insecure_private_key -o
IdentityFile=~/.vagrant.d/insecure_private_key -o IdentityFile=~/.
vagrant.d/insecure_private_key -o IdentityFile=~/.vagrant.d/insecure_
private_key -o ControlMaster=auto -o ControlPersist=60s' ansible-playbook
--connection=ssh --timeout=30 --extra-vars="ansible_ssh_user='vagrant'"
--limit="domaincontrollers" --inventory-file=ansible/test.ini -vvvv
ansible/plays/domaincontroller.yml
Using /Users/sharepointoscar/git-repos/vagrant-ansible-packer-spfarm/
ansible.cfg as config file
statically included: /Users/sharepointoscar/git-repos/vagrant-ansible-packer-
spfarm/ansible/roles/internal/domaincontroller/tasks/promote-domain.yml
statically included: /Users/sharepointoscar/git-repos/vagrant-ansible-packer-
spfarm/ansible/roles/internal/domaincontroller/tasks/create-ad-accounts.yml
Loading callback plugin default of type stdout, v2.0 from /usr/local/
Cellar/ansible/2.3.1.0/libexec/lib/python2.7/site-packages/ansible/plugins/
callback/__init__.pyc

PLAYBOOK: domaincontroller.yml
************************************************
1 plays in ansible/plays/domaincontroller.yml

PLAY [domaincontroller.yml | All roles]
**************************************
```

```
TASK [Gathering Facts]
***************************************************
Using module file /usr/local/Cellar/ansible/2.3.1.0/libexec/lib/python2.7/
site-packages/ansible/modules/windows/setup.ps1
<192.168.2.19> ESTABLISH WINRM CONNECTION FOR USER: vagrant on PORT 5985 TO
192.168.2.19
EXEC (via pipeline wrapper)
ok: [DomainController1]
META: ran handlers

TASK [domaincontroller : Set DNS Server]
*************************************
task path: /Users/sharepointoscar/git-repos/vagrant-ansible-packer-spfarm/
ansible/roles/internal/domaincontroller/tasks/promote-domain.yml:2
<192.168.2.19> ESTABLISH WINRM CONNECTION FOR USER: vagrant on PORT 5985 TO
192.168.2.19
EXEC (via pipeline wrapper)
EXEC (via pipeline wrapper)
<192.168.2.19> PUT "/Users/sharepointoscar/git-repos/vagrant-
ansible-packer-spfarm/ansible/roles/internal/domaincontroller/
files/SetDNS.ps1" TO "C:\Users\vagrant\AppData\Local\Temp\ansible-
tmp-1509936795.34-13173498082809\SetDNS.ps1"
EXEC (via pipeline wrapper)
EXEC (via pipeline wrapper)
changed: [DomainController1] => {
    "changed": true,
    "rc": 0,
    "stderr": "",
    "stdout": "\r\n\r\n__GENUS          : 2\r\n__CLASS          :
__PARAMETERS\r\n__SUPERCLASS     : \r\n__DYNASTY          : __PARAMETERS\
r\n__RELPATH: \r\n__PROPERTY_COUNT : 1\r\n__DERIVATION     : {}\r\n
__SERVER          : \r\n__NAMESPACE      : \r\n__PATH          : \r\
nReturnValue      : 0\r\nPSComputerName   : \r\n\r\n\r\n\r\n",
    "stdout_lines": [
        "",
        "",
        "__GENUS          : 2",
```

```
        "__CLASS          : __PARAMETERS",
        "__SUPERCLASS     : ",
        "__DYNASTY        : __PARAMETERS",
        "__RELPATH        : ",
        "__PROPERTY_COUNT : 1",
        "__DERIVATION     : {}",
        "__SERVER         : ",
        "__NAMESPACE      : ",
        "__PATH           : ",
        "ReturnValue      : 0",
        "PSComputerName   : ",
        "",
        "",
        ""
    ]
}
```

```
TASK [domaincontroller : Install Active Directory on Windows Server 2016]
******
task path: /Users/sharepointoscar/git-repos/vagrant-ansible-packer-spfarm/
ansible/roles/internal/domaincontroller/tasks/promote-domain.yml:5
<192.168.2.19> ESTABLISH WINRM CONNECTION FOR USER: vagrant on PORT 5985 TO
192.168.2.19
EXEC (via pipeline wrapper)
EXEC (via pipeline wrapper)
<192.168.2.19> PUT "/Users/sharepointoscar/git-repos/vagrant-
ansible-packer-spfarm/ansible/roles/internal/domaincontroller/files/
create-domain.ps1" TO "C:\Users\vagrant\AppData\Local\Temp\ansible-
tmp-1509936813.45-54504785903488\create-domain.ps1"
EXEC (via pipeline wrapper)
EXEC (via pipeline wrapper)
changed: [DomainController1] => {
    "changed": true,
    "rc": 0,
    "stderr": "",
    "stdout": "Configuring SharePoint Farm Active Directory Domain
```

Controller\r\n \r\nThe task has completed successfully.
\r\nSee log %windir%\\security\\logs\\scesrv.log for detail info.
\r\nCompleted 5 percent (0/18)   \tProcess Security Policy area
\r\nCompleted 22 percent (3/18)   \tProcess Security Policy area
\r\nCompleted 44 percent (7/18)   \tProcess Security Policy area
\r\nCompleted 61 percent (10/18)   \tProcess Security Policy area
\r\nCompleted 77 percent (13/18)   \tProcess Security Policy area
\r\nCompleted 100 percent (18/18) \tProcess Security Policy area
\r\n \r\nThe task has completed successfully.\r\nSee log
%windir%\\security\\logs\\scesrv.log for detail info.\r\n\r\nSuccess
RestartNeeded FeatureResult \r\n
------- ------------- -------------
\r\n   True   No {Active Directory Domain Services,
Group PolicyManagement, Remote Server Administration Tools...\r\n
                \r\nchanged\r\n\r\n\r\n",
    "stdout_lines": [
        "Configuring SharePoint Farm Active Directory Domain Controller",
        "   ",
        "The task has completed successfully.",
        "See log %windir%\\security\\logs\\scesrv.log for detail info.",
        "Completed 5 percent (0/18)   \tProcess Security Policy area ",
        "Completed 22 percent (3/18)   \tProcess Security Policy area ",
        "Completed 44 percent (7/18)   \tProcess Security Policy area ",
        "Completed 61 percent (10/18)   \tProcess Security Policy area ",
        "Completed 77 percent (13/18)   \tProcess Security Policy area ",
        "Completed 100 percent (18/18) \tProcess Security Policy area ",
        "   ",
        "The task has completed successfully.",
        "See log %windir%\\security\\logs\\scesrv.log for detail info.",
        "",
        "Success RestartNeeded FeatureResult",
        "------- ------------- -------------",
        "   True   No {Active Directory Domain Services,
        Group Policy Management, Remote Server Administration Tools...",
        "",
        "changed",

```
        "",
        ""

    ]
}
TASK [domaincontroller : win_reboot]
*************************************
task path: /Users/sharepointoscar/git-repos/vagrant-ansible-packer-
spfarm/ansible/roles/internal/domaincontroller/tasks/promote-domain.yml:11
<192.168.2.19> ESTABLISH WINRM CONNECTION FOR USER: vagrant on PORT 5985
TO 192.168.2.19
EXEC (via pipeline wrapper)
attempting post-reboot test command 'whoami'
<192.168.2.19> ESTABLISH WINRM CONNECTION FOR USER: vagrant on PORT 5985 TO
192.168.2.19
EXEC (via pipeline wrapper)
changed: [DomainController1] => {
    "changed": true,
    "rebooted": true,
    "warnings": []
}

TASK [domaincontroller : debug]
***********************************************
task path: /Users/sharepointoscar/git-repos/vagrant-ansible-packer-spfarm/
ansible/roles/internal/domaincontroller/tasks/promote-domain.yml:15
ok: [DomainController1] => {
    "msg": "The result of the reboot is: True"
}
......
```

You will notice that this is very verbose. This is because in our Vagrantfile, we indicated that Ansible be verbose by specifying it within our provisioner (see the bold text in the following).

```
    # Use specific Ansible Playbooks and other provisioners based on SP
    Machine Role
    if role == 'DomainController'
      cfg.vm.provision :ansible do |ansible|
```

```
#let's configure the domain controler and add
# a) the SP Service Accounts
# b) Sample User Accounts
ansible.limit = "domaincontrollers"
ansible.playbook = "ansible/plays/domaincontroller.yml"
ansible.inventory_path = "ansible/test.ini"
ansible.verbose = "vvvv"
ansible.raw_ssh_args = ANSIBLE_RAW_SSH_ARGS
end
```

As you move down the output, you can see that each subtask is being executed and what the results are.

Bring up the SharePoint Vagrant Environment

Having hostnames in place allows us to execute Vagrant commands targeting a specific box. For example, if we wanted to only bring up and configure the domain server, we would execute the following command.

```
$ vagrant up DomainController1
```

Vagrant only brings up the box named DomainController1 and runs our Ansible and ServerSpec provisioners specified in the Vagrantfile. If we want to check the status of all the machines in our farm, we execute the following command.

```
$ vagrant status
```

This outputs something similar to the following.

```
Current machine states:

DomainController1          not created (virtualbox)
WFE1                       not created (virtualbox)
Database1                  not created (virtualbox)
AppServer1                 not created (virtualbox)

This environment represents multiple VMs. The VMs are all listed
above with their current state. For more information about a specific
VM, run `vagrant status NAME`.
```

As you can see, the environment is not up at this time. So let's bring this environment up.

Bring up the Domain Controller

First, we want to bring up the domain controller, since all other servers depend on this role. Hence, this is why we indicate in `vagrant-machines.yaml` that this role is the default. This ensures that Vagrant brings it up first.

Executing the following command brings up our domain controller.

```
$ vagrant up DomainController1
```

In the background, Vagrant is configuring the base Windows Server 2016 and promoting it to a domain controller. Ansible tasks are then executed to add the SharePoint Server service accounts and other user accounts. We use DomainController1 because that is the name we gave our Vagrant box in the YAML file.

Should this command fail, destroy the machine by running the following command.

```
$ vagrant destroy -f DomainController1
```

Then, try to bring up the DomainController1 machine again.

Tip   Ensure that you have installed the ServerSpec provisioner so that the command runs successfully. If you have not installed it, simply comment out lines 120 to 122, where the ServerSpec tests are called for the domain controller build.

The Ansible Tasks

Each server in the topology has a specific role; therefore, we want to configure each machine differently based on that role. For our Ansible directory structure, we've included an Ansible role that matches each SharePoint role, as shown in the following directory structure.

```
> $ tree -L 2
├── Database
│       ├── defaults
│       ├── files
│       ├── handlers
│       ├── meta
│       ├── tasks
```

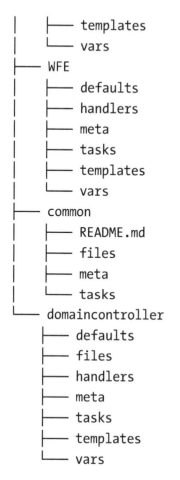

```
│   ├── templates
│   └── vars
├── WFE
│   ├── defaults
│   ├── handlers
│   ├── meta
│   ├── tasks
│   ├── templates
│   └── vars
├── common
│   ├── README.md
│   ├── files
│   ├── meta
│   └── tasks
└── domaincontroller
    ├── defaults
    ├── files
    ├── handlers
    ├── meta
    ├── tasks
    ├── templates
    └── vars

27 directories, 1 file
```

You can see we have the database, the domain controller, and a WFE role (the app server role is not shown). If you take a closer look, each Ansible role has a tasks folder, in which we define the various tasks for provisioning and configuration management.

The tasks folder contains a main.yaml file, which includes as many YAML files as we want. These represent grouped tasks. For this role, we have two tasks: promote-domain.yml and create-ad-accounts.yml, which ensure that all SharePoint service accounts are created, as well as sample user accounts.

```
> $ tree -L 2
├── defaults
│   └── main.yml
├── files
│   ├── ImportADServiceAccounts.ps1
```

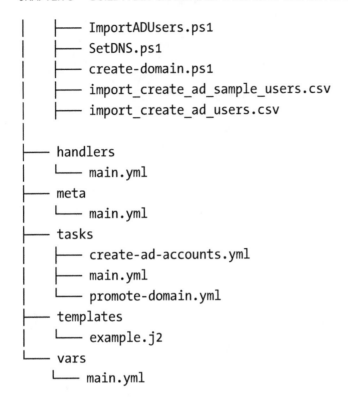

```
|       ├── ImportADUsers.ps1
|       ├── SetDNS.ps1
|       ├── create-domain.ps1
|       ├── import_create_ad_sample_users.csv
|       ├── import_create_ad_users.csv
|
├── handlers
|       └── main.yml
├── meta
|       └── main.yml
├── tasks
|       ├── create-ad-accounts.yml
|       ├── main.yml
|       └── promote-domain.yml
├── templates
|       └── example.j2
└── vars
        └── main.yml

7 directories, 15 files
```

For the domain controller, we ensure that the following happens:

- Promote Windows Server 2016 to domain controller

- Reboot server after promoting it to domain controller

- Add the Vagrant user account to domain admins

- Create SharePoint service accounts

- Create sample user accounts

Tip   You can change the service account names and user accounts, which all reside in their respective CSV files within the domain controller role located at ansible/roles/internal/domaincontroller/files.

The main.yml file includes the tasks that we want to ensure are executed on the playbook. The file contents look like Listing 3-4.

Listing 3-4. main.yml Includes Tasks to Be Executed on the Playbook

```
---
  - include: promote-domain.yml
  - include: create-ad-accounts.yml
```

Let's take a closer look at the first task, which handles promoting a simple Windows Server 2016 into a domain controller. The following is what our task looks like.

```
- name: Install Active Directory on Windows Server 2016
  script: files/create-domain.ps1
  register: script_result
  changed_when: "'changed' in script_result.stdout"
  tags:
    - create-domain
- name: Reboot for AD changes to take effect.
  win_reboot:
  tags:
    - create-domain
- name: Server is rebooted, now a domain controller. Stop all other tasks
without failing or errors.
  meta: end_play
  tags:
    - create-domain
```

You will notice that there are braces with variables on some of our task files. These come from the Ansible group vars YAML file, which is located under `Ansible/group_vars/all/all.yml`.

Ansible looks at these variables every time it executes a playbook or task. Listing 3-5 shows the contents of the group vars `all.yml` file, which contains all of our global variables.

Listing 3-5. The all.yml file Contents with Global Variables Used by Ansible

```
----
domain: "sposcar.local"
network: "10.0.2.15"
netbios: "SPOSCAR"
```

```
dns_server: "192.168.2.19"
domain_admin_user: packer@sposcar.local
domain_admin_password: pass@word1!
ansible_user: vagrant
ansible_password: vagrant
ansible_port: 5985
ansible_connection: winrm
ansible_winrm_transport: ntlm
ansible_winrm_operation_timeout_sec: 120
ansible_winrm_read_timeout_sec: 150

# The following is necessary for Python 2.7.9+ (or any older Python that
has backported SSLContext, eg, Python 2.7.5 on RHEL7) when using default
WinRM self-signed certificates:
ansible_winrm_server_cert_validation: ignore

#SharePoint related global variables
SharePointBitsPath: "c:\\SP\\2016\\SharePoint"
SharePointPrerequisitesPath: "c:\\SP\\2016\\prerequisiteinstallerfiles"

cloud_host: null
```

Note   Though not necessary, you may want to change the domain name and
other variables in this file to meet your needs and to deploy your own test/dev
environment locally.

Let's go through the contents of the promote-domain.yml file in detail.

The first Ansible task promotes the machine as a domain controller. This is also
handled by a PowerShell script, which resides within the files folder of the Ansible role.

```
- name: Install Active Directory on Windows Server 2016
  script: files/create-domain.ps1
  register: script_result
  changed_when: "'changed' in script_result.stdout"
  tags:
    - create-domain
```

Note   We intentionally used a PowerShell script to show how you might do this. However, you can use the Ansible win_domain module as well, and this task can easily be modified to use it.

We then initiate a reboot.

```
- name: Reboot for AD changes to take effect.
  win_reboot:
  tags:
    - create-domain
```

Next, we end the playbook execution.

```
- name: Server is reboot, now a domain controller. Stop all other tasks
without failing or errors.
  meta: end_play
  tags:
    - create-domain
```

Tip   We used tags in each Ansible task. We go over this in detail later in this chapter, and show you how we use them to only execute tasks with specific tags.

Using Ansible to Execute Playbooks or Specific Tasks

Although our Vagrantfile uses the Ansible provisioner, there may be times when we want to run a playbook or even a specific task after the machines have been provisioned. This is where the power of Ansible continues to shine.

For our scenario, we've already built our domain controller. If you recall, there are two main ansible tasks. We've covered one, promote-domain.yml. Now let's assume that we want to run our second task—create-ad-accounts.yml—manually to populate the Active Directory with SharePoint service accounts and sample domain user accounts.

From the root of our GitHub repository directory, we execute the following command.

```
> $ ansible-playbook -i ansible/test.ini ansible/plays/domaincontroller.yml
--extra-vars="ansible_user='vagrant@sposcar.local' ansible_password='Pass@
word1!'" --start-at-task="Add Admin Account to Domain Admins" -vvvvv
```

There is a lot of useful information in this command. First, at the end of the command, we specify which task from the playbook Ansible should start at. In this case, it is Add Admin Account to Domain Admins. We must pass several parameters contained within–extra-vars, which include the credentials that Ansible should use for the WinRM connection to the Windows server.

Tip   Once the server is promoted to a domain controller, we must use the domain account when executing future Ansible tasks. In this case, it is vagrant@sposcar. local, which is in the domain admins group. It was added to the administrators group as well.

The output of executing the command is as follows.

```
$ ansible-playbook -i ansible/hosts_dev_env.yaml ansible/plays/
domaincontroller.yml --extra-vars="ansible_user='vagrant@sposcar.local'
ansible_password='vagrant'" --start-at-task="Ensure vagrant is member of
Domain Admins, Administrators, Domain Users" -vvvv
Using /Users/sharepointoscar/git-repos/vagrant-ansible-packer-spfarm/
ansible.cfg as config file
statically included: /Users/sharepointoscar/git-repos/vagrant-ansible-packer-
spfarm/ansible/roles/internal/domaincontroller/tasks/promote-domain.yml
statically included: /Users/sharepointoscar/git-repos/vagrant-ansible-packer-
spfarm/ansible/roles/internal/domaincontroller/tasks/create-ad-accounts.yml
Loading callback plugin default of type stdout, v2.0 from /usr/local/
Cellar/ansible/2.3.1.0/libexec/lib/python2.7/site-packages/ansible/plugins/
callback/__init__.pyc

PLAYBOOK: domaincontroller.yml
********************************************************************************
1 plays in ansible/plays/domaincontroller.yml

PLAY [domaincontroller.yml | All roles]
********************************************************************************
TASK [Gathering Facts]
********************************************************************************
Using module file /usr/local/Cellar/ansible/2.3.1.0/libexec/lib/python2.7/
site-packages/ansible/modules/windows/setup.ps1
```

```
<192.168.2.19> ESTABLISH WINRM CONNECTION FOR USER: vagrant@sposcar.local
on PORT 5985 TO 192.168.2.19
EXEC (via pipeline wrapper)
ok: [DomainController1]

TASK [domaincontroller : Add Admin Account to Domain Admins]
********************************************************
task path: /Users/sharepointoscar/git-repos/vagrant-ansible-packer-spfarm/
ansible/roles/internal/domaincontroller/tasks/create-ad-accounts.yml:21
Using module file/usr/local/Cellar/ansible/2.3.1.0/libexec/lib/python2.7/
site-packages/ansible/modules/windows/win_user.ps1
<192.168.2.19> ESTABLISH WINRM CONNECTION FOR USER: vagrant@sposcar.local
on PORT 5985 TO 192.168.2.19
EXEC (via pipeline wrapper)
changed: [DomainController1] => {
    "account_disabled": false,
    "account_locked": false,
    "changed": true,
    "description": "Vagrant User",
    "fullname": "Vagrant",
    "groups": [
        {
            "name": "Domain Users",
            "path": "WinNT://SPOSCAR/SP2012R2AD/Domain Users"
        },
        {
            "name": "Domain Admins",
            "path": "WinNT://SPOSCAR/SP2012R2AD/Domain Admins"
        },
        {
            "name": "Administrators",
            "path": "WinNT://SPOSCAR/SP2012R2AD/Administrators"
        }
    ],
    "name": "vagrant",
    "password_expired": false,
    "password_never_expires": true,
```

```
    "path": "WinNT://SPOSCAR/SP2012R2AD/vagrant",
    "sid": "S-1-5-21-2574927426-235769873-4243624142-1000",
    "state": "present",
    "user_cannot_change_password": false
}

TASK [domaincontroller : Create directory structure]
****************************************************************************
task path: /Users/sharepointoscar/git-repos/vagrant-ansible-packer-spfarm/
ansible/roles/internal/domaincontroller/tasks/create-ad-accounts.yml:31
Using module file /usr/local/Cellar/ansible/2.3.1.0/libexec/lib/python2.7/
site-packages/ansible/modules/windows/win_file.ps1
<192.168.2.19> ESTABLISH WINRM CONNECTION FOR USER: vagrant@sposcar.local
on PORT 5985 TO 192.168.2.19
EXEC (via pipeline wrapper)
ok: [DomainController1] => {
    "changed": false
}

TASK [domaincontroller : Copy ImportADUsers.ps1 to c:\tmp]
****************************************************************************
task path: /Users/sharepointoscar/git-repos/vagrant-ansible-packer-spfarm/
ansible/roles/internal/domaincontroller/tasks/create-ad-accounts.yml:37
Using module file /usr/local/Cellar/ansible/2.3.1.0/libexec/lib/python2.7/
site-packages/ansible/modules/windows/win_stat.ps1
<192.168.2.19> ESTABLISH WINRM CONNECTION FOR USER: vagrant@sposcar.local
on PORT 5985 TO 192.168.2.19
EXEC (via pipeline wrapper)
EXEC (via pipeline wrapper)
EXEC (via pipeline wrapper)
<192.168.2.19> PUT "/Users/sharepointoscar/git-repos/vagrant-
ansible-packer-spfarm/ansible/roles/internal/domaincontroller/files/
ImportADUsers.ps1" TO "C:\Users\vagrant\AppData\Local\Temp\ansible-
tmp-1511718603.79-192615989626036\source"
Using module file /usr/local/Cellar/ansible/2.3.1.0/libexec/lib/python2.7/
site-packages/ansible/modules/windows/win_copy.ps1
EXEC (via pipeline wrapper)
```

```
changed: [DomainController1] => {
    "changed": true,
    "checksum": "0724159ad9d191ca52e0623fadbd29fc5b993140",
    "dest": "c:\\tmp\\ImportADUsers.ps1",
    "operation": "file_copy",
    "original_basename": "source",
    "size": 1095,
    "src": "C:\\Users\\vagrant\\AppData\\Local\\Temp\\ansible-
tmp-1511718603.79-192615989626036\\source"
}

TASK [domaincontroller : Copy ImportADServiceAccounts.ps1 to c:\tmp]
************************************************************************
task path: /Users/sharepointoscar/git-repos/vagrant-ansible-packer-spfarm/
ansible/roles/internal/domaincontroller/tasks/create-ad-accounts.yml:43
Using module file /usr/local/Cellar/ansible/2.3.1.0/libexec/lib/python2.7/
site-packages/ansible/modules/windows/win_stat.ps1
<192.168.2.19> ESTABLISH WINRM CONNECTION FOR USER: vagrant@sposcar.local
on PORT 5985 TO 192.168.2.19
EXEC (via pipeline wrapper)
EXEC (via pipeline wrapper)
EXEC (via pipeline wrapper)
<192.168.2.19> PUT "/Users/sharepointoscar/git-repos/vagrant-
ansible-packer-spfarm/ansible/roles/internal/domaincontroller/files/
ImportADServiceAccounts.ps1" TO "C:\Users\vagrant\AppData\Local\Temp\
ansible-tmp-1511718606.71-55782215012245\source"
Using module file /usr/local/Cellar/ansible/2.3.1.0/libexec/lib/python2.7/
site-packages/ansible/modules/windows/win_copy.ps1
EXEC (via pipeline wrapper)
changed: [DomainController1] => {
    "changed": true,
    "checksum": "9abba9699cf28836bf1d297faad25e2686916977",
    "dest": "c:\\tmp\\ImportADServiceAccounts.ps1",
    "operation": "file_copy",
    "original_basename": "source",
```

```
    "size": 1122,
    "src": "C:\\Users\\vagrant\\AppData\\Local\\Temp\\ansible-
        tmp-1511718606.71-55782215012245\\source"
}
TASK [domaincontroller : Copy import_create_ad_sample_users.csv to c:\tmp]
*************************************************************************
task path: /Users/sharepointoscar/git-repos/vagrant-ansible-packer-spfarm/
ansible/roles/internal/domaincontroller/tasks/create-ad-accounts.yml:49
Using module file /usr/local/Cellar/ansible/2.3.1.0/libexec/lib/python2.7/
site-packages/ansible/modules/windows/win_stat.ps1
<192.168.2.19> ESTABLISH WINRM CONNECTION FOR USER: vagrant@sposcar.local
on PORT 5985 TO 192.168.2.19
EXEC (via pipeline wrapper)
EXEC (via pipeline wrapper)
EXEC (via pipeline wrapper)
<192.168.2.19> PUT "/Users/sharepointoscar/git-repos/vagrant-ansible-
packer-spfarm/ansible/roles/internal/domaincontroller/files/import_create_
ad_sample_users.csv" TO "C:\Users\vagrant\AppData\Local\Temp\ansible-
tmp-1511718609.85-26838732258466\source"
Using module file /usr/local/Cellar/ansible/2.3.1.0/libexec/lib/python2.7/
site-packages/ansible/modules/windows/win_copy.ps1
EXEC (via pipeline wrapper)
changed: [DomainController1] => {
    "changed": true,
    "checksum": "f23522a391042e12beed481e26b3ce750d110994",
    "dest": "c:\\tmp\\import_create_ad_sample_users.csv",
    "operation": "file_copy",
    "original_basename": "source",
    "size": 584,
    "src": "C:\\Users\\vagrant\\AppData\\Local\\Temp\\ansible-tmp-
    1511718609.85-26838732258466\\source"
}
```

```
TASK [domaincontroller : Copy import_create_ad_users.csv to c:\tmp]
**********************************************************************
task path: /Users/sharepointoscar/git-repos/vagrant-ansible-packer-spfarm/
ansible/roles/internal/domaincontroller/tasks/create-ad-accounts.yml:55
Using module file /usr/local/Cellar/ansible/2.3.1.0/libexec/lib/python2.7/
site-packages/ansible/modules/windows/win_stat.ps1
<192.168.2.19> ESTABLISH WINRM CONNECTION FOR USER: vagrant@sposcar.local
on PORT 5985 TO 192.168.2.19
EXEC (via pipeline wrapper)
EXEC (via pipeline wrapper)
EXEC (via pipeline wrapper)
<192.168.2.19> PUT "/Users/sharepointoscar/git-repos/vagrant-ansible-
packer-spfarm/ansible/roles/internal/domaincontroller/files/import_
create_ad_users.csv" TO "C:\Users\vagrant\AppData\Local\Temp\ansible-
tmp-1511718613.09-193282785092701\source"
Using module file /usr/local/Cellar/ansible/2.3.1.0/libexec/lib/python2.7/
site-packages/ansible/modules/windows/win_copy.ps1
EXEC (via pipeline wrapper)
changed: [DomainController1] => {
    "changed": true,
    "checksum": "5216a8ccb14780492685c34a8015def573b19439",
    "dest": "c:\\tmp\\import_create_ad_users.csv",
    "operation": "file_copy",
    "original_basename": "source",
    "size": 589,
    "src": "C:\\Users\\vagrant\\AppData\\Local\\Temp\\ansible-
          tmp-1511718613.09-193282785092701\\source"
}

TASK [domaincontroller : Create AD User Accounts]
**********************************************************************
task path: /Users/sharepointoscar/git-repos/vagrant-ansible-packer-spfarm/
ansible/roles/internal/domaincontroller/tasks/create-ad-accounts.yml:62
Using module file /usr/local/Cellar/ansible/2.3.1.0/libexec/lib/python2.7/
site-packages/ansible/modules/windows/win_shell.ps1
<192.168.2.19> ESTABLISH WINRM CONNECTION FOR USER: vagrant@sposcar.local
on PORT 5985 TO 192.168.2.19
```

```
EXEC (via pipeline wrapper)
changed: [DomainController1] => {
    "changed": true,
    "cmd": "C:\\tmp\\ImportADUsers.ps1",
    "delta": "0:00:01.703369",
    "end": "2017-11-26 05:50:17.917848",
    "rc": 0,
    "start": "2017-11-26 05:50:16.214478",
    "stderr": "",
    "stderr_lines": [],
    "stdout": "",
    "stdout_lines": []
}

TASK [domaincontroller : Create SharePoint AD Service Accounts]
*********************************************************************************
task path: /Users/sharepointoscar/git-repos/vagrant-ansible-packer-spfarm/
ansible/roles/internal/domaincontroller/tasks/create-ad-accounts.yml:66
Using module file /usr/local/Cellar/ansible/2.3.1.0/libexec/lib/python2.7/
site-packages/ansible/modules/windows/win_shell.ps1
<192.168.2.19> ESTABLISH WINRM CONNECTION FOR USER: vagrant@sposcar.local
on PORT 5985 TO 192.168.2.19
EXEC (via pipeline wrapper)
changed: [DomainController1] => {
    "changed": true,
    "cmd": "C:\\tmp\\ImportADServiceAccounts.ps1",
    "delta": "0:00:01.358956",
    "end": "2017-11-26 05:50:19.917204",
    "rc": 0,
    "start": "2017-11-26 05:50:18.558247",
    "stderr": "",
    "stderr_lines": [],
    "stdout": "",
    "stdout_lines": []
}
META: ran handlers
META: ran handlers
```

```
PLAY RECAP
*****************************************************************************
DomainController1          : ok=9    changed=7    unreachable=0    failed=0
```

As you can see, nine tasks completed successfully and zero failed. Great! If we were to run this command again, tasks would not change anything because nothing changed on the server side. This is called *idempotence*.

Tip   Idempotence is the property of certain operations in mathematics and computer science that can be applied multiple times without changing the result beyond. In the context of managing systems, you can think of it as ensure you check the state of resources and only change them if is not in the desired state.

We now have a populated Active Directory with SharePoint service accounts and sample user accounts. We've made a lot of progress. Our domain controller spins up properly and Active Directory has the required service accounts for SharePoint. Why not make that a test when spinning up the domain controller role?

In the next section, we use ServerSpec to write some basic tests to check for these things. This is a great start for when we are ready to incorporate our build into a CI/CD environment. Imagine, once your tests pass, you can publish the Vagrantfile into source control for developers to access the fully working version.

But first, let's bring up our database server, which serves as the back end for the SharePoint 2016 farm.

Bring up the Database Server

Now that our domain controller is provisioned, let's bring up our database server. The database server also has its own Ansible role, which handles these two key tasks:

- Joining the database server to the domain

- Executing an unattended SQL Server 2014 installation (this takes at least five minutes, so do not panic if it seems as if the task is stuck)

Much like the domain server, we can easily provision the database server by executing the following command.

```
>$ vagrant up Database1
```

The Vagrantfile ensures that the Ansible playbook is executed when the machine is provisioned. The playbook is located at `ansible/plays/databaseservers.yml`. The playbook tasks are located in the respective role at `ansible/roles/internal/database/tasks/main.yml`.

The contents of the `main.yml` look similar to the following:

```
- include: join-to-domain.yml
- include: mountimg.yml
```

As you can see, there are two main tasks for our database playbook. Let's go over each one in detail.

The Ansible Tasks

This task ensures that the database server is joined to the domain we have created. The key subtask uses an Ansible built-in module, `win_domain_membership`, and we configure it as follows to join the database server to our domain.

Listing 3-6. The join-to-domain.yml Task

```
- name: Join Database to Domain Controller
  win_domain_membership:
      dns_domain_name: "{{domain}}"
      hostname: "SP2016SQLSERVER"
      domain_admin_user: "{{domain_admin_user}}"
      domain_admin_password: "{{domain_admin_password}}"
      state: domain
  register: domain_state
  tags:
    - join-to-domain
    - all-environments
- name: Reboot server after joining to Domain Server
  win_reboot:
  when: domain_state.reboot_required
  tags:
  - join-to-domain
  - all-environments
```

Note that we are using the hostname provided by our `vagrant-machines.yml` file. We use the domain admin and password, as we need proper rights to join this machine to the domain. And we use our global variables, which have curly braces. These come from our `ansible/group_vars/all/all.yml` file. Lastly, we reboot the machine so that changes can take effect.

The mountimg.yml Task

Now that we've joined the server to our domain and restarted it, we focus on the unattended installation of SQL Server 2014. `ansible/roles/internal/database/tasks/mountimg.yml` contains the entire group of tasks that are needed to achieve this. Listing 3-7 is what it looks like in its entirety.

Listing 3-7. The Contents of the mountimg.yml Task File

```
- name: Disable User Access Control UAC
  script: ../roles/internal/common/files/disable-uac.bat
  tags:
  - vagrant-environment

- name: Install .NET Framework 3.5 (its required for database install)
  win_feature:
    name: Net-Framework-Features
    state: present
    restart: yes
    include_sub_features: yes
    include_management_tools: yes
  tags:
  - vagrant-environment
# open up firewall port 1433 for SQL to accept incoming connections.
- name: Open port 1433 for remote connections to SQL Server
  win_firewall_rule:
      name: SQL Server Remote Connections
      localport: 1433
      action: allow
      direction: in
      protocol: tcp
```

```
      profiles: domain,private,public
      state: present
      enabled: yes
  tags:
  - all-environments

# since we are using Ansible 2.4, change this to the built-in module
- name: Add SPOSCAR\SP_FARM to Local Admins Group
  script: ../../common/files/AddDomainAccountToAdminsGroup.ps1 -domain_
  username SPOSCAR\SP_FARM -domain_username_password pass@word1!
  tags:
  - all-environments

- name: Add SPOSCAR\administrator to Local Admins Group
  script: ../../common/files/AddDomainAccountToAdminsGroup.ps1 -domain_
  username SPOSCAR\Administrator  -domain_username_password pass@word1!
  tags:
  - all-environments

- name: Add SPOSCAR\vagrant to SysAdmin SQL Role (return 0 = success)
  win_shell: sqlcmd -S SP2016SQLSERVER -Q "EXEC sp_addsrvrolemember
  'SPOSCAR\vagrant', 'sysadmin';"
  tags:
  - all-environments

- name: Reboot Server so UAC changes take effect.
  win_reboot:

- name: Download SQL Server ISO to root C:\
  win_get_url:
    url: http://download.microsoft.com/download/6/D/9/6D90C751-6FA3-4A78-
    A78E-D11E1C254700/SQLServer2014SP2-FullSlipstream-x64-ENU.iso
    dest: c:\SQLServer2014-x64-ENU.iso
    force: no
  tags:
  - vagrant-environment
```

```
- name: Copy SQL Server ConfigurationFile to C:\
  win_copy:
    src: ../roles/internal/Database/files/ConfigurationFile.ini
    dest: c:\ConfigurationFile.ini
  tags:
  - vagrant-environment

- name: Mount SQL Server ISO Image
  win_disk_image:
   image_path: C:\SQLServer2014-x64-ENU.iso
   state: present
  register: disk_image_out
  tags:
  - vagrant-environment

- name: Output debug info for path mount
  debug:
    msg: 'The path to SQL executable {{ disk_image_out.mount_path }}setup.
    exe'
  tags:
  - vagrant-environment

#Run a command under a non-Powershell interpreter (cmd in this case)
- name: Run SQL Server unattended setup command using ConfigurationFile
  win_shell: D:\setup.exe /Q /ConfigurationFile=c:\ConfigurationFile.ini
  args:
    executable: cmd
  tags:
  - vagrant-environment
```

Several things are happening here. First, we make sure that UAC is disabled because it would prevent the install otherwise. We then install the .NET Framework. The only reason this may be needed is because the installation uses some .NET assemblies to carry out the install as a workflow. We ensure that port 1433 is open because SQL Server uses this for remote connections.

Next, we ensure that the SP farm accounts are in the local administrator's group.

```
- name: Add SPOSCAR\SP_FARM to Local Admins Group
  script: ../../common/files/AddDomainAccountToAdminsGroup.ps1 -domain_
  username SPOSCAR\SP_FARM -domain_username_password pass@word1!
  tags:
  - all-environments
- name: Add SPOSCAR\administrator to Local Admins Group
  script: ../../common/files/AddDomainAccountToAdminsGroup.ps1 -domain_
  username SPOSCAR\Administrator  -domain_username_password pass@word1!
  tags:
  - all-environments
```

We then download the SQL binaries using the following subtask.

```
- name: Download SQL Server ISO to root C:\
  win_get_url:
    url: http://download.microsoft.com/download/6/D/9/6D90C751-6FA3-4A78-
    A78E-D11E1C254700/SQLServer2014SP2-FullSlipstream-x64-ENU.iso
    dest: c:\SQLServer2014-x64-ENU.iso
    force: no
  tags:
  - vagrant-environment
```

Note   We reuse these tasks to build the SharePoint farm in Azure and AWS;
therefore, we use tags to execute only the tasks needed for a given environment.

This subtask is at the core of the playbook to execute an unattended SQL install.

Once the SQL image is downloaded, we mount the disc and then execute the installation via a configuration file.

```
# Run a command under a non-Powershell interpreter (cmd in this case)
- name: Run SQL Server unattended setup command using ConfigurationFile
  win_shell: D:\setup.exe /Q /ConfigurationFile=c:\ConfigurationFile.ini
  args:
    executable: cmd
```

> **Note** This task may take up to 10 minutes. As a rule of thumb, if you don't see an error on the Ansible console, do not stop the task, because it is actually working.

There is a lengthy output once the subtask has completed. We've removed most of it. Highlight the output you need to discover if it was successful. This is Setup result: 0.

Listing 3-8. The Output Shows "Setup result:0" Which Indicates A Successful SQL Server Unattended Install

```
[......]
"----------------------------------------------------------------------",
        "Running Action: CloseUI",
        "Stop action skipped in UI Mode Quiet",
        "Completed Action: CloseUI, returned True",
        "Completed Action: ExecuteCloseWorkflow, returned True",
        "Completed Action: ExecuteCompleteWorkflow, returned True",
        "",
        ,
        "",
        ,
        "---------------------------------------------------------------",
        "",
        ,
        "Setup result: 0",
        "SQM Service: Sqm does not have active session.",
        "Microsoft (R) SQL Server 2014 12.00.2000.08",
        "",
        ,
        "Copyright (c) Microsoft Corporation. All rights reserved.",
        "",
        ,
        ""

    ]
}
```

Bring up the WFE and App Server

Now that our domain controller and database server are up and running, we want to bring up our WFE and app server using Vagrant (similar to what we did for the domain controller). The WFE role has different tests we will run, and has different Ansible task as well. However, both app server and WFE use the same Ansible tasks.

Noteworthy are the Ansible tasks that handle the actual installation of SharePoint 2016, and we will go through it in detail. Let's bring up the server by running the following command.

```
>$ vagrant up WFE1
```

Vagrant executes the Ansible provisioner at the time the WFE is brought up, and runs the corresponding Ansible playbook located at `ansible/plays/webservers.yml`. The playbook looks at the WFE role tasks, which are located under `ansible/roles/internal/WFE/tasks/main.yml`. It is in the file where we specify which tasks should be executed and in what order. The following is what the file looks like.

```
---

 - include: join-to-domain.yml
 - include: mount-sp-img.yml
```

As of the writing of this book, the `include` directive was deprecated; it still works, but you will see warnings. For information on using `import_tasks`, see `https://docs.ansible.com/ansible/2.4/playbooks_reuse_includes.html`.

Note   The SharePoint roles are dictated by the SPAutoInstaller XML configuration file, where we specify the topology for the farm. SPAutoInstaller uses the hostname to assign roles. We defined our hostnames in our vagrant-machines.yaml file on the root of our GitHub project repository.

As you can see, we only have two main tasks for the WFE role. Here is the overall expected end state:

- The WFE should be joined to the domain server.

- The SharePoint image disk should be mounted.

- SharePoint 2016 prerequisites should be downloaded.

- SharePoint 2016 prerequisites should be installed.

- SPAutoInstaller is triggered and the farm is created and configured as per the XML file within our Git repository at `ansible/roles/common/files/SPAutoInstaller/SPAutoInstallerInput.xml`.

Tip   If you wish to view the contents of the SPAutoInstallInput.xml file, simply go to `http://spautoinstaller.com` and upload it to view the configuration, change as desired, and then download and include in the GitHub repository.

The join-to-domain.yml Task

Tip   Recall that the variable values shown in braces come from the group_vars/all/all.yml Ansible file. Also, notice that we reuse a task from the domain controller Ansible role, based on the following SetDNS.ps1 file location.

Let's take a closer look at the first task: `join-to-domain.yml`. As you probably guessed, this task's sole purpose is to join the machine to the domain controller we provisioned earlier in this chapter. The task uses built-in Ansible modules such as the `win_domain_membership`, which makes it easy to join the machine to our domain. Here is a closer look at our task file. The first subtask handles the actual joining to the domain. This subtask uses a built-in module called `win_domain_membership`. We use additional variables, such as the `domain_admin_user` and `domain_admin_password`, for the proper rights to join the machine to the `sposcar.local` domain.

```
- name: Join Webserver to Domain Controller
  win_domain_membership:
      dns_domain_name: "{{domain}}"
      hostname: "{{cloud_host}}"
      domain_admin_user: "{{domain_admin_user}}"
      domain_admin_password: "{{domain_admin_password}}"
      state: domain
  register: domain_state
  tags:
    - join-to-domain

- name: Reboot server after joining to Domain Server
  win_reboot:
```

```
when: domain_state.reboot_required
tags:
  - join-to-domain
```

Once the server is joined, a reboot ensures that things work properly.

The mount-sp-img.yml Task

This task is used to do several things, such as downloading the SharePoint prerequisites, installing prerequisites, mounting the SharePoint Server disc, and initiating the SPAutoInstaller script.

Tip   If you wish to see the SPAutoInstaller in action while the task is executing, simply log in using the vagrant@sposcar.local account before the SPAutoInstaller script is triggered. You should be able to view the various PowerShell and DOS windows cycling through the process.

Listing 3-9 shows the contents of the task file; most of the subtasks are self-explanatory. We will focus on the last task.

Listing 3-9. The mount-sp-img.yml file Contains Subtasks, Including the SharePoint Install Task

```
- name: Install PSExec
  win_chocolatey:
    name: psexec
  ignore_errors: yes

- name: Download SharePoint 2016
  win_get_url:
    url: https://download.microsoft.com/download/0/0/4/004EE264-7043-45BF-
    99E3-3F74ECAE13E5/officeserver.img
    dest: c:\
    force: no

# This task mounts the Officeserver.img file
- name: Mount the SharePoint Bits IMG
```

```
    win_disk_image:
        image_path: c:\officeserver.img
        state: present
    register: disk_image_out

- name: Create c:\SP directory
  win_file:
    path: C:\SP
    state: directory

- name: Copy SP folder (SPAutoInstaller folder structure)
  win_copy:
    src: ../../common/files/SP/
    dest: C:\SP
    force: false

- name: Copy SP Bits in {{ disk_image_out.mount_path }} to SPAutoInstaller
        folder structure
  win_shell: XCOPY {{ disk_image_out.mount_path }}\* C:\SP\2016\SharePoint\
  /s /i /Y
  args:
  executable: cmd

- name: Install All Required Windows Features
  win_feature:
    name: NET-HTTP-Activation,NET-Non-HTTP-Activ,NET-WCF-Pipe-
    Activation45,NET-WCF-HTTP-Activation45,Web-Server,Web-WebServer,Web-
    Common-Http,Web-Static-Content,Web-Default-Doc,Web-Dir-Browsing,Web-
    Http-Errors,Web-App-Dev,Web-Asp-Net,Web-Asp-Net45,Web-Net-Ext,Web-
    Net-Ext45,Web-ISAPI-Ext,Web-ISAPI-Filter,Web-Health,Web-Http-
    Logging,Web-Log-Libraries,Web-Request-Monitor,Web-Http-Tracing,Web-
    Security,Web-Basic-Auth,Web-Windows-Auth,Web-Filtering,Web-Digest-
    Auth,Web-Performance,Web-Stat-Compression,Web-Dyn-Compression,Web-Mgmt-
    Tools,Web-Mgmt-Console,Web-Mgmt-Compat,Web-Metabase,WAS,WAS-Process-
    Model,WAS-NET-Environment,WAS-Config-APIs,Web-Lgcy-Scripting,Windows-
    Identity-Foundation,Xps-Viewer
    state: present
    restart: yes
```

```yaml
    include_sub_features: yes
    include_management_tools: yes
  register: feature_result

# make sure to put the prerequisites in the proper folder.
- name: Download SharePoint Prerequisites
  script: ../../common/files/DownloadPrerequisites.ps1 -SPPrerequisitesPath
  {{SharePointPrerequisitesPath}}

- name: Install SharePoint Prerequisites via PowerShell
  script: ../../common/files/Install-Prerequisites.ps1 -SharePointBitsPath
  {{SharePointBitsPath}}

- name: Reboot after Installing Prerequisites
  win_reboot:

- name: Trigger AutoSPInstaller (computer will restart and continue
  install)
  win_psexec:
    command: C:\SP\AutoSPInstaller\AutoSPInstallerLaunch.bat
    priority: high
    elevated: yes
    interactive: yes
    username: sposcar\vagrant
    password: Pass@word1!
    wait: no

# Pause for 5 minutes to build app cache.
- name: Wait for SPAutoInstaller to Finish first pass
  pause:
    minutes: 5

- name: Reboot server for AutoSPInstaller to continue
  win_reboot:

- name: wait until admin port 2016 is available. start checking after 15
  minutes.
  win_wait_for:
    port: 2016
```

```
state: present
delay: 900
sleep: 20
timeout: 1800
```

The last task, `Trigger AutoSPInstaller (computer will restart and continue install)`, performs the heavy lifting when it comes to installing the SharePoint bits and configuring the farm.

As you can see, it uses a batch file called `AutoSPInstallerLaunch.bat`. If we wanted to see what is happening on the server, we simply sign in using the domain account SPOSCAR\vagrant on the VirtualBox VM.

We call PSExec with specific parameters and flags to ensure that the batch runs.

Tip   If you feel that the last task, Trigger AutoSPInstaller, is taking a while, you can sign in to the VirtualBox using the SPOSCAR\vagrant domain account. The task manager indicates which PowerShell tasks are running. Signing in typically triggers the AutoSPInstaller to continue installing if it was stuck for some reason, at least from our experience with running the Ansible playbook.

In our `mount-sp-img.yml` file, we have a subtask to install PSExec because we use PSExec to ensure that it is called properly since we are executing it via a different machine (in this case, a MacBook Pro with Ansible installed).

Using ServerSpec to Test SharePoint Server Role Config

Testing infrastructure is important in achieving the desired state to replicate (in this scenario, the SharePoint development environment). Running infrastructure test scripts can be done through the Vagrant ServerSpec provisioner and running tests manually. Integrating these kinds of tests into the CI/CD pipeline is ideal when we start automating our infrastructure testing, and we want to automatically publish the Vagrantfile to GitHub, for example.

About ServerSpec

ServerSpec is an open source framework that helps with testing infrastructure, a practice known as test-driven infrastructure (TDI). ServerSpec is built on top of Rspec, which typically is used to test Ruby applications while practicing test-driven development (TDD).

About Test-Driven Infrastructure

For many years, IT pros managed infrastructure manually and with a combination of ad hoc scripts to deploy updates to servers by literally remoting into the machine using RDP and installing software updates or packages. This created inconsistency and did not allow for a repeatable process in deploying similar machine images for a given application. Needless to say, maintenance of these systems became a nightmare.

When we think of the benefits that TDD has brought to developers, we start realizing those same benefits are applicable when we treat our infrastructure as code and incorporate testing into the deployment of infrastructure on-premises and to the cloud.

By treating infrastructure as code, we start leveraging source control for managing our infrastructure, we enable multiple team members to contribute to the infrastructure, and we gain consistency and a repeatable process for managing resources. Infrastructure as Code is relatively new, and many clouds are using it. For example, you can easily programmatically build an entire virtual private cloud on AWS using tools like Terraform.

Tip   Later in this book, we go over how to use Terraform to deploy a SharePoint farm to AWS and Azure clouds.

Running Tests on Provisioning VM

For our scenario, we will execute tests against the domain controller. These are specific to this role. For example, we do not want IIS running on the domain controller. We also want to make sure that the WinRM and RDP ports are open. Lastly, we want to make sure that the server is configured as a domain controller. You can find the tests on our solution at `/spec/SP2012R2AD.sposcar.local/sample_spec.rb`, where you can also augment additional tests, as you see fit.

At times, you may be required to run tests shortly after the environment is up and running or has been provisioned by Vagrant. To do this, you need to install an open source plug-in Vagrant-Serverspec by executing the following command.

```
> $ vagrant plugin install vagrant-serverspec –plugin-version "1.0.1"
```

Next, you need to modify the Vagrantfile to run the tests after the virtual machine has been provisioned. In our scenario, it is the domain controller (see Listing 3-10).

Listing 3-10. Add Serverspec Provisioner and Specify a Test to Run

```
    # Use specific Ansible Playbooks and other provisioners based on SP
    Machine Role
if role == 'DomainController'
  cfg.vm.provision :ansible do |ansible|
      #let's configure the domain controler and add
      # a) the SP Service Accounts
      # b) Sample User Accounts
      ansible.limit = "domaincontrollers"
      ansible.playbook = "ansible/plays/domaincontroller.yml"
      ansible.inventory_path = "ansible/test.ini"
      ansible.verbose = "vvvv"
      ansible.raw_ssh_args = ANSIBLE_RAW_SSH_ARGS
  end
  # Run ServerSpec Tests for Domain Controller
  cfg.vm.provision :serverspec do |spec|
    spec.pattern = 'spec/SP2013R2AD.sposcar.local/sample_spec.rb'
  end
elsif role == 'Front-End'
```

The code listed in bold is what we need to add to our Vagrantfile, roughly starting on line 105. If all goes well, you should see the output or test results in your terminal, similar to the following output.

```
 Port "5985"
   should be listening

Port "3389"
   should be listening
```

```
Command "Get-ExecutionPolicy"
  stdout
    should match /RemoteSigned/
  exit_status     should eq 0

Windows feature "AD-Domain-Services"
  should be installed by "powershell"

Windows feature "IIS-Webserver"
  should not be installed by "dism"

Windows feature "Web-Webserver"
  should not be installed by "powershell"

Finished in 5.69 seconds (files took 0.87226 seconds to load)
7 examples, 0 failures
```

Running Tests Manually

There may be times when you want to manually run your infrastructure tests. Since we have provisioned the domain controller, we can execute a command to quickly run our tests as shown in Listing 3-11.

Caution The Rakefile at the root of the project uses a dev.env file that contains the credentials to pass the WinRM connection. You must change these values if you are not using the sposcar.local domain and have modified the corresponding Ansible playbook and group_vars. Please ensure that the group_vars/all.yml domain admin and domain password match the credentials on the dev environment; otherwise, tests will fail.

Listing 3-11. Command to Run Tests Manually and Output Shown

```
> $ bundle exec rake spec
/Users/sharepointoscar/.rvm/rubies/ruby-2.3.4/bin/ruby -I/Users/
sharepointoscar/.rvm/gems/ruby-2.3.4/gems/rspec-core-3.7.0/lib:/Users/
sharepointoscar/.rvm/gems/ruby-2.3.4/gems/rspec-support-3.7.0/lib /Users/
sharepointoscar/.rvm/gems/ruby-2.3.4/gems/rspec-core-3.7.0/exe/rspec
--pattern spec/shared/\*_spec.rb
```

No examples found.

Finished in 0.0004 seconds (files took 0.07191 seconds to load)
0 examples, 0 failures

/Users/sharepointoscar/.rvm/rubies/ruby-2.3.4/bin/ruby -I/Users/
sharepointoscar/.rvm/gems/ruby-2.3.4/gems/rspec-core-3.7.0/lib:/Users/
sharepointoscar/.rvm/gems/ruby-2.3.4/gems/rspec-support-3.7.0/lib /Users/
sharepointoscar/.rvm/gems/ruby-2.3.4/gems/rspec-core-3.7.0/exe/rspec
--pattern spec/SP2012R2AD.sposcar.local/*_spec.rb

Port "5985"
  should be listening

Port "3389"
  should be listening

User "SPOSCAR\vagrant"
  should exist
  should belong to group "Administrators"

User "SPOSCAR\vagrant"
  should exist
  should belong to group "SPOSCAR\\Domain Admins"

Command "Get-ExecutionPolicy"
  stdout
    should match /RemoteSigned/
  exit_status
    should eq 0

Windows feature "AD-Domain-Services"
  should be installed by "powershell"

Windows feature "IIS-Webserver"
  should not be installed by "dism"

Windows feature "Web-Webserver"
  should not be installed by "powershell"

Finished in 8.06 seconds (files took 0.49515 seconds to load)
11 examples, 0 failures

```
/Users/sharepointoscar/.rvm/rubies/ruby-2.3.4/bin/ruby -I/Users/
sharepointoscar/.rvm/gems/ruby-2.3.4/gems/rspec-core-3.7.0/lib:/Users/
sharepointoscar/.rvm/gems/ruby-2.3.4/gems/rspec-support-3.7.0/lib /Users/
sharepointoscar/.rvm/gems/ruby-2.3.4/gems/rspec-core-3.7.0/exe/rspec
--pattern spec/sp2016WFE/\*_spec.rb
No examples found.

Finished in 0.00045 seconds (files took 0.37396 seconds to load)
0 examples, 0 failures
```

Because this is a domain controller, we want to ensure that it does not have IIS running. We also want to ensure that the vagrant account is a member of the domain admins group, and, of course, that this server is a domain controller.

The command executes all tests for all the spec files located under the spec/ folder. A successful execution shows the output in green, but you can also see the number of failures and successes within the output shown.

Testing Additional Server Roles

You can add servers to test by executing a serverspec-init command (on Ubuntu, you can simply run serverspec-init), as follows:

```
> $ bundle exec serverspec-init
Select OS type:

  1) UN*X
  2) Windows
Select number: 2

Select a backend type:

  1) WinRM
  2) Cmd (local)

Select number: 1

Input target host name: sp2016WFE
 + spec/sp2016WFE/
 + spec/sp2016WFE/sample_spec.rb
 + spec/spec_helper.rb
!! Rakefile already exists and differs from template
```

As you can see, a new folder under `spec/` is added with the hostname that we specified. Now that this folder structure is in place, we can start adding our tests to the `sample_spec.rb` file, which we can rename to `wfe_spec.rb`, for example.

Tip   In the next chapter, we implement CI using Jenkins as our Packer template, which outputs the Vagrant `.box` file needed to build our SharePoint 2016 dev environment.

Push Vagrantfile to GitHub

The Vagrantfile is part of the overall GitHub project repository. So anytime we make changes, we can easily push those to GitHub by checking our code and pushing those changes—at which point, all developers on the team get the latest and greatest solution that they can use to quickly build the SharePoint 2016 dev environment.

One key component to this workflow is that after checking in the latest version of the Vagrantfile, a continuous integration server, such as Jenkins, should be used to build this environment continuously and run the tests; and if those tests pass, tag the repo with the appropriate release.

Summary

In this chapter, we walked through building a Vagrant SharePoint dev environment and discussed the configuration management aspect of it. On the configuration management side, we used Ansible to execute various playbooks and tasks against the corresponding SharePoint VM role to install and configure the SharePoint VM. We also discussed how to incorporate infrastructure driven testing, and walked through some basic spec tests using ServerSpec to test our domain controller at the time of provisioning the VM.

In the next chapter, we create the proper artifacts in Packer, run them through CI using Jenkins, and deploy our SharePoint 2016 farm to AWS in a staging environment. The key benefit is that we are using the same Packer template that we used for standing up the Vagrant dev environment to mirror the environment configuration.

CHAPTER 4

Provisioning the SharePoint Farm to Azure Using Terraform

In this chapter, we will go through the exercise of using Infrastructure as Code (IaC) to deploy the SharePoint 2016 farm to a staging environment in the Azure cloud. We do this by using one of the most sought after and reliable tools out on the market—Terraform by HashiCorp. Before coding our infrastructure, we will code our Packer image template to target Azure RM. The end result of our Packer exercise will be a VHD image that we can use in Terraform to build our SharePoint virtual machines.

About the Solution Architecture

This architecture includes a custom Azure image deployed by us. The design leverages a gallery Azure image that contains SQL Server 2014 preinstalled. Other servers in the topology use the custom Azure image that we built using Packer (see Figure 4-1).

© Oscar Medina, Ethan Schumann 2018
O. Medina and E. Schumann, *DevOps for SharePoint*, https://doi.org/10.1007/978-1-4842-3688-8_4

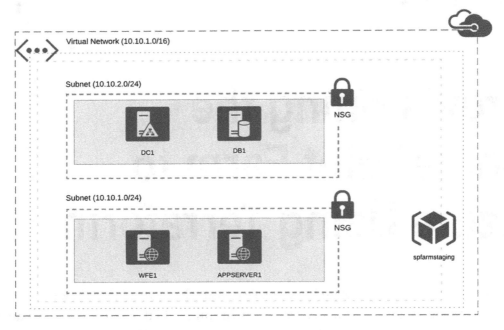

Figure 4-1. *The SharePoint 2016 farm topology in Azure cloud*

Note   In Chapter 2, we introduced you to the various open source tools, including Terraform. This book is not meant to be an exhaustive resource, but rather assumes you know the basics. A book can be written just on Terraform, and it has been written. We recommend James Turnbull's *The Terraform Book* (Turnbull Press, 2016). For information on how Terraform works, please visit `www.terraform.io`.

Terraform Folder Structure

Our Terraform folder is divided into environments. We have AWS and Azure, local, and a shared folder. The shared folder is where common artifacts are used by any environment. Items such as the SSH keys and providers reside within this folder.

```
> $ tree terraform -l 2
terraform
├── aws
│   ├── environments
│   │   ├── development
│   │   │   └── backend.tf
│   │   └── staging
│   │       ├── ad.tf
│   │       ├── backend.tf
│   │       ├── eip.tf
│   │       ├── gateways.tf
│   │       ├── iam_roles.tf
│   │       ├── main.tf
│   │       ├── ssm.tf
│   │       └── variables.tf
│   ├── keypair.tf
│   ├── output.tf
│   ├── scripts
│   │   ├── EC2-Windows-Launch.zip
│   │   ├── change_hostname.ps1
│   │   ├── create-bucket.sh
│   │   └── install_EC2_Launch.ps1
│   ├── terraform.tfstate.backup
│   └── variables.tf
├── azure
│   └── environments
│       └── staging
│           ├── backend.tf
│           ├── beconf.tfvars
│           ├── main.tf
│           ├── terraform.tfvars
│           ├── variables.tf
│           └── vms.tf
├── local
│   └── variables.tf
└── shared
```

```
├── providers
│   ├── aws.tf
│   └── azure.tf
└── ssh_keys
    ├── keys.tf
    ├── spfarm_rsa.pem
    └── spfarm_rsa.pub
2 [error opening dir]
```

12 directories, 29 files

For the purpose of going through the deployment of the SharePoint 2016 farm to Azure, we will mainly focus on the Azure folder contents within our GitHub repository throughout this exercise.

We will be building a fully functional SharePoint 2016 staging environment in Azure. First, we need to create our "golden image" and add it to a blob storage along other artifacts. We do this using a custom Bash script described in the next section.

Create Base VM Image Using Packer

As with our development environment in Chapter 3, we'll use Packer to create our base image for the Vagrant development environment farm. The process is similar to Azure; we use Packer to build the image. But first, we must set up proper credentials, storage account, container, and so forth, to hold the image or VHD and connect to Azure via Packer.

To do this, we have a Bash script that handles all of this for us, rather than our doing it manually via the Azure portal. Who wants to do things manually when automation is at the core of practicing DevOps, right?

Note   The azure_setup.sh script was originally part of the repository found at https://github.com/SharePointOscar/packer/blob/master/contrib/azure-setup.sh, which is a fork from the HashiCorp/Packer repository. A pull request was merged as of the writing of this book, but we included the script within our repo for convenience in the /packer/azure-scripts folder. We updated it to use the latest Azure CLI. The script ensures the required software is installed on your machine.

Running the Bash Script

Our Bash script is located under the packer/azure-scripts/azure-setup.sh location. The script checks for required software in order to run successfully. It creates all the required resources including a service principal, application, storage account, and assigns the "owner" role to our service principal to run Packer.

Tip   The output of the script is used by our configuration in Ansible, Packer, and Terraform, we will update those accordingly as we go through the exercise.

We execute our script and respond to the required parameters as needed. Next, we break down what the script does section by section.

Checking for Required Software

As shown next, the Bash script, once executed, ensures that we have the Azure CLI and jq (https://stedolan.github.io/jq), a lightweight JSON processor that easily filters results from Azure CLI commands.

Tip   For information on installing Azure CLI and other tools, please see Chapter 2.

```
$ ./azure-setup.sh setup
Found az-cli version: azure-cli (2.0.23)

acr (2.0.17)
acs (2.0.22)
advisor (0.1.0)
appservice (0.1.22)
backup (1.0.3)
batch (3.1.7)
batchai (0.1.3)
billing (0.1.6)
cdn (0.0.10)
cloud (2.0.10)
cognitiveservices (0.1.9)
command-modules-nspkg (2.0.1)
```

```
configure (2.0.12)
consumption (0.2.0)
container (0.1.15)
core (2.0.23)
cosmosdb (0.1.15)
dla (0.0.15)
dls (0.0.18)
eventgrid (0.1.5)
extension (0.0.6)
feedback (2.0.6)
find (0.2.7)
interactive (0.3.11)
iot (0.1.15)
keyvault (2.0.15)
lab (0.0.13)
monitor (0.0.13)
network (2.0.19)
nspkg (3.0.1)
profile (2.0.16)
rdbms (0.0.9)
redis (0.2.10)
reservations (0.1.0)
resource (2.0.19)
role (2.0.15)
servicefabric (0.0.7)
sql (2.0.17)
storage (2.0.21)
vm (2.0.20)

Python location '/usr/local/opt/python3/bin/python3.6'
Extensions directory '/Users/sharepointoscar/.azure/cliextensions'

Python (Darwin) 3.6.4 (default, Jan  3 2018, 12:27:11)
[GCC 4.2.1 Compatible Apple LLVM 9.0.0 (clang-900.0.39.2)]

Legal docs and information: aka.ms/AzureCliLegal
Found jq version: jq-1.5
```

Using Device Authentication with Azure CLI

Next, our script prompts us with a URL that we must visit, and then we enter the generated code. Once we do this, we see the output on the terminal window as follows. If we previously signed in using the Azure CLI, then we can simply hit Enter, and the script will use the default account.

```
To sign in, use a web browser to open the page https://aka.ms/devicelogin
and enter the code <GENERATED CODE> to authenticate.
[
  {
    "cloudName": "AzureCloud",
    "id": "eeec2e47-bae1-eeeb-a35a-35a7adc3e293",
    "isDefault": true,
    "name": "Microsoft Azure Enterprise",
    "state": "Enabled",
    "tenantId": "555c7f71-4542-4e9b-8e1a-99e4751f4750",
    "user": {
      "name": "account@mycompany.com",
      "type": "user"
    }
  }
]
[
  {
    "cloudName": "AzureCloud",
    "id": "eeec2e47-bae1-eeeb-a35a-35a7adc3e293",
    "isDefault": true,
    "name": "Microsoft Azure Enterprise",
    "state": "Enabled",
    "tenantId": "555c7f71-4542-4e9b-8e1a-99e4751f4750",
    "user": {
      "name": "me@mycompany.com",
      "type": "user"
    }
  }
]
```

```
Please enter the Id of the account you wish to use. If you do not see
a valid account in the list press Ctrl+C to abort and create one.
If you leave this blank we will use the Current account.
>
Using subscription_id: <redacted>
Using tenant_id: <redacted>
ukwest
```

Specify a Unique Name for Storage Account, Resource Group, and Client

Next, our script prompts us to type a unique name to create multiple resources needed such as the storage account and resource group. For our purposes in this exercise, we provided the value spfarmstaging.

```
Choose a name for your resource group, storage account and client
client. This is arbitrary, but it must not already be in use by
any of those resources. ALPHANUMERIC ONLY. Ex: mypackerbuild
> spfarmstaging
```

Application Secret

Part of the Azure setup requires the OAuth authentication against Azure Active Directory. For this reason, we must create an application. Our script will provide us both the client_id and client_secret once we run it completely.

```
Enter a secret for your application. We recommend generating one with
openssl rand -base64 24. If you leave this blank we will attempt to
generate one for you using openssl. THIS WILL BE SHOWN IN PLAINTEXT.
Ex: mypackersecret8734
> pass@word1!
[
  {
    "displayName": "East Asia",
    "id": "/subscriptions/<redacted>/locations/eastasia",
    "latitude": "22.267",
    "longitude": "114.188",
```

```
    "name": "eastasia",
    "subscriptionId": null
  },

...
  {
    "displayName": "Korea South",
    "id": "/subscriptions/<redacted>/locations/koreasouth",
    "latitude": "35.1796",
    "longitude": "129.0756",
    "name": "koreasouth",
    "subscriptionId": null
  }
]
```

Choose a Location

Much like AWS has regions, Azure has the equivalent: locations. We are on the West Coast, so we choose "westus". The script was not too clear on what you needed to enter. Be sure to enter the internal name of the location, as shown next.

```
Choose which region your resource group and storage account will be
created. example: westus
> westus
==> Creating resource group
{
  "id": "/subscriptions/<redacted>/resourceGroups/spfarmstaging",
  "location": "westus",
  "managedBy": null,
  "name": "spfarmstaging",
  "properties": {
    "provisioningState": "Succeeded"
  },
  "tags": null
}
==> Creating storage account
{
```

```
"accessTier": null,
"creationTime": "2018-01-28T14:57:12.552228+00:00",
"customDomain": null,
"enableHttpsTrafficOnly": false,
"encryption": {
  "keySource": "Microsoft.Storage",
  "keyVaultProperties": null,
  "services": {
    "blob": {
      "enabled": true,
      "lastEnabledTime": "2018-01-28T14:57:12.583446+00:00"
    },
    "file": {
      "enabled": true,
      "lastEnabledTime": "2018-01-28T14:57:12.583446+00:00"
    },
    "queue": null,
    "table": null
  }
},
"id": "/subscriptions/<redacted>/resourceGroups/spfarmstaging/providers/
Microsoft.Storage/storageAccounts/spfarmstaging",
"identity": null,
"kind": "Storage",
"lastGeoFailoverTime": null,
"location": "westus",
"name": "spfarmstaging",
"networkRuleSet": {
  "bypass": "AzureServices",
  "defaultAction": "Allow",
  "ipRules": [],
  "virtualNetworkRules": []
},
"primaryEndpoints": {
  "blob": "https://spfarmstaging.blob.core.windows.net/",
```

```
    "file": "https://spfarmstaging.file.core.windows.net/",
    "queue": "https://spfarmstaging.queue.core.windows.net/",
    "table": "https://spfarmstaging.table.core.windows.net/"
  },
  "primaryLocation": "westus",
  "provisioningState": "Succeeded",
  "resourceGroup": "spfarmstaging",
  "secondaryEndpoints": {
    "blob": "https://spfarmstaging-secondary.blob.core.windows.net/",
    "file": null,
    "queue": "https://spfarmstaging-secondary.queue.core.windows.net/",
    "table": "https://spfarmstaging-secondary.table.core.windows.net/"
  },
  "secondaryLocation": "eastus",
  "sku": {
    "capabilities": null,
    "kind": null,
    "locations": null,
    "name": "Standard_RAGRS",
    "resourceType": null,
    "restrictions": null,
    "tier": "Standard"
  },
  "statusOfPrimary": "available",
  "statusOfSecondary": "available",
  "tags": {},
  "type": "Microsoft.Storage/storageAccounts"
}
==> Creating application
==> Does application exist?
==> application does not exist
==> Creating service principal
f9da43fa-8ed6-4584-9250-10d2c682a434 was selected.
==> Creating permissions

Sleeping for 10 seconds to wait for resources to be
```

created. If you get an error about a resource not existing, you can try increasing the amount of time we wait after creating resources by setting PACKER_SLEEP_TIME to something higher than the default.

```
==> Creating permissions
{
  "id": "/subscriptions/<redacted>/providers/Microsoft.Authorization/
roleAssignments/a4671417-6abf-4308-987a-914cc9c77ae0",
  "name": "a4671417-6abf-4308-987a-914cc9c77ae0",
  "properties": {
    "additionalProperties": {
      "createdBy": null,
      "createdOn": "2018-01-28T14:57:52.5603878Z",
      "updatedBy": "c3923ccf-8eb1-4aa5-90a0-96efa181866a",
      "updatedOn": "2018-01-28T14:57:52.5603878Z"
    },
    "principalId": "f9da43fa-8ed6-4584-9250-10d2c682a434",
    "roleDefinitionId": "/subscriptions/<redacted>/providers/Microsoft.
    Authorization/roleDefinitions/8e3af657-a8ff-443c-a75c-2fe8c4bcb635",
    "scope": "/subscriptions/<redacted>"
  },
  "type": "Microsoft.Authorization/roleAssignments"
}
```

Successful Script Output

The following output is critical for configuring both the Packer template and the Terraform later in this chapter. We will configure Packer in the next section with this information.

Tip   Use the following output for configuration of the Packer template. These values will also be useful for our Ansible and Terraform configuration later in this chapter. If you get warnings, this is fine, generally, and you can proceed.

```
{
        "client_id": "454547cb-2e0f-420b-b526-4f3b1c7d09c9",
        "client_secret": "pass@word1!",
        "object_id": "v9Ca43fa-8ed6-4584-9250-10d2c682a434",
        "subscription_id": "<redacted>",
        "tenant_id": "<redacted>",
        "resource_group_name": "spfarmstaging",
        "storage_account": "spfarmstaging",
}
```

Please note that it is a best practice to place this sensitive data in environment variables. For reference, please refer to www.packer.io/docs/templates/user-variables.html for details.

Create Packer Image VM

To create our Azure VM image using Packer, we must have a Packer JSON template. Our file is located at the following location on our repo: packer/azure_windows2016.

The Packer Template for Azure

The following are the contents of our template. We need to modify the variable values to match the values provided from the output when we ran azure_setup.sh. We have highlighted in bold the section we pasted from the output of running the Bash script.

```
{

  "builders": [{
    "type": "azure-arm",

    "client_id": "0b4547cb-2e0f-420b-b526-4f3b1c7d09c9",
    "client_secret": "pass@word1!",
    "object_id": "f9da43fa-8ed6-4584-9250-10d2c682a434",
    "subscription_id": "dbbc2e47-bae1-4b8b-a35a-35a7adc3e293",
    "tenant_id": "484c7f71-4542-4e8b-8e1a-87e4751f4750",
    "resource_group_name": "spfarmstaging",
    "storage_account": "spfarmstaging",
```

```
    "capture_container_name": "images",
    "capture_name_prefix": "packer",

    "os_type": "Windows",
    "image_publisher": "MicrosoftWindowsServer",
    "image_offer": "WindowsServer",
    "image_sku": "2016-Datacenter",

    "communicator": "winrm",
    "winrm_use_ssl": "true",
    "winrm_insecure": "true",
    "winrm_timeout": "3m",
    "winrm_username": "packer",

    "azure_tags": {
        "environment": "Staging",
        "task": "Image deployment"
    },

    "location": "West US",
    "vm_size": "Standard_DS2_v2"
  }],
    "provisioners": [{
            "type": "powershell",
            "inline": [
                "& $env:SystemRoot\\System32\\Sysprep\\Sysprep.exe /oobe /
                generalize /quiet /quit",
                "while($true) { $imageState = Get-ItemProperty HKLM:\\
                SOFTWARE\\Microsoft\\Windows\\CurrentVersion\\Setup\\State
                | Select ImageState; if($imageState.ImageState -ne 'IMAGE_
                STATE_GENERALIZE_RESEAL_TO_OOBE') { Write-Output $imageState.
                ImageState; Start-Sleep -s 10   } else { break } }"
            ]
        }]
}
```

Of special interest, is the provisioners section, where we execute a PowerShell command to Sysprep and generalize the machine. Listing 4-1 is the full output of the successful Packer build command.

Tip   Please modify the metadata as needed. For example, you may deploy the Packer template to a different location than West US by simply modifying that value.

Listing 4-1. Successful Output Would Include the Information Shown

```
me@sharepointoscar ~/git-repos/vagrant-ansible-packer-spfarm/packer
> $ packer build azure_windows_2016.json

==> azure-arm: Running builder ...
    azure-arm: Creating Azure Resource Manager (ARM) client ...
==> azure-arm: Creating resource group ...
==> azure-arm:   -> ResourceGroupName : 'packer-Resource-Group-1m34k3fnm8'
==> azure-arm:   -> Location          : 'West US'
==> azure-arm:   -> Tags              :
==> azure-arm:   ->> environment : Staging
==> azure-arm:   ->> task : Image deployment
==> azure-arm: Validating deployment template ...
==> azure-arm:   -> ResourceGroupName : 'packer-Resource-Group-1m34k3fnm8'
==> azure-arm:   -> DeploymentName    : 'pkrdp1m34k3fnm8'
==> azure-arm: Deploying deployment template ...
==> azure-arm:   -> ResourceGroupName : 'packer-Resource-Group-1m34k3fnm8'
==> azure-arm:   -> DeploymentName    : 'pkrdp1m34k3fnm8'
==> azure-arm: Getting the certificate's URL ...
==> azure-arm:   -> Key Vault Name        : 'pkrkv1m34k3fnm8'
==> azure-arm:   -> Key Vault Secret Name : 'packerKeyVaultSecret'
==> azure-arm:   -> Certificate URL       : 'https://pkrkv1m34k3fnm8.vault.
azure.net/secrets/packerKeyVaultSecret/648567e836a74c8bbb7c3d44f9a311bc'
==> azure-arm: Setting the certificate's URL ...
==> azure-arm: Validating deployment template ...
==> azure-arm:   -> ResourceGroupName : 'packer-Resource-Group-1m34k3fnm8'
```

```
==> azure-arm:  -> DeploymentName     : 'pkrdp1m34k3fnm8'
==> azure-arm: Deploying deployment template ...
==> azure-arm:  -> ResourceGroupName : 'packer-Resource-Group-1m34k3fnm8'
==> azure-arm:  -> DeploymentName     : 'pkrdp1m34k3fnm8'
==> azure-arm: Getting the VM's IP address ...
==> azure-arm:  -> ResourceGroupName  : 'packer-Resource-Group-1m34k3fnm8'
==> azure-arm:  -> PublicIPAddressName : 'packerPublicIP'
==> azure-arm:  -> NicName            : 'packerNic'
==> azure-arm:  -> Network Connection : 'PublicEndpoint'
==> azure-arm:  -> IP Address         : '104.42.225.145'
==> azure-arm: Waiting for WinRM to become available...
==> azure-arm: Connected to WinRM!
==> azure-arm: Provisioning with Powershell...
==> azure-arm: Provisioning with shell script: /var/folders/c2/qf2pd13d4fs4
jhsthhlf4gr40000gn/T/packer-powershell-provisioner046129632
    azure-arm: #< CLIXML
    azure-arm: IMAGE_STATE_COMPLETE
    azure-arm: IMAGE_STATE_UNDEPLOYABLE
    azure-arm: IMAGE_STATE_UNDEPLOYABLE
    azure-arm: IMAGE_STATE_UNDEPLOYABLE
    azure-arm: IMAGE_STATE_UNDEPLOYABLE
    azure-arm: IMAGE_STATE_UNDEPLOYABLE
    azure-arm: IMAGE_STATE_UNDEPLOYABLE
    azure-arm: IMAGE_STATE_UNDEPLOYABLE
    azure-arm: IMAGE_STATE_UNDEPLOYABLE
    azure-arm: IMAGE_STATE_UNDEPLOYABLE
    azure-arm: <Objs Version="1.1.0.1" xmlns="http://schemas.microsoft.com/
    powershell/2004/04"><Obj S="progress" RefId="0">
    <TN RefId="0"><T>System.Management.Automation.PSCustomObject
    </T><T>System.Object</T></TN><MS><I64 N="SourceId">1</I64><PR
    N="Record"><AV>Preparing modules for first use.</AV><AI>0</AI><Nil
    /><PI>-1</PI><PC>-1</PC><T>Completed</T><SR>-1</SR><SD> </SD></PR>
    </MS></Obj></Objs>
==> azure-arm: Querying the machine's properties ...
==> azure-arm:  -> ResourceGroupName : 'packer-Resource-Group-1m34k3fnm8'
```

```
==> azure-arm:   -> ComputeName        : 'pkrvm1m34k3fnm8'
==> azure-arm:   -> OS Disk             : 'https://spfarmstaging.blob.core.
                                          windows.net/images/pkros1m34k3fnm8.
                                          vhd'
==> azure-arm: Powering off machine ...
==> azure-arm:   -> ResourceGroupName : 'packer-Resource-Group-1m34k3fnm8'
==> azure-arm:   -> ComputeName        : 'pkrvm1m34k3fnm8'
==> azure-arm: Capturing image ...
==> azure-arm:   -> ResourceGroupName : 'packer-Resource-Group-1m34k3fnm8'
==> azure-arm:   -> ComputeName        : 'pkrvm1m34k3fnm8'
==> azure-arm: Deleting resource group ...
==> azure-arm:   -> ResourceGroupName : 'packer-Resource-Group-1m34k3fnm8'
==> azure-arm: Deleting the temporary OS disk ...
==> azure-arm:   -> OS Disk : 'https://spfarmstaging.blob.core.windows.net/
                               images/pkros1m34k3fnm8.vhd'
Build 'azure-arm' finished.

==> Builds finished. The artifacts of successful builds are:
--> azure-arm: Azure.ResourceManagement.VMImage:

StorageAccountLocation: westus
OSDiskUri: https://spfarmstaging.blob.core.windows.net/system/Microsoft.
Compute/Images/spfarmstaging/packer-osDisk.30ec65ab-39ed-43a2-b6c4-
62e0dc5b5cf6.vhd
OSDiskUriReadOnlySas: https://spfarmstaging.blob.core.windows.net/system/
Microsoft.Compute/Images/spfarmstaging/packer-osDisk.30ec65ab-39ed-43a2-
b6c4-62e0dc5b5cf6.vhd?se=2018-02-28T15%3A31%3A58Z&sig=erjQA27JuVFHk4qwdpFIg
wiuXDTdgkB%2BKLHHnRU2YR4%3D&sp=r&sr=b&sv=2015-02-21
TemplateUri: https://spfarmstaging.blob.core.windows.net/system/Microsoft.
Compute/Images/spfarmstaging/packer-vmTemplate.30ec65ab-39ed-43a2-b6c4-
62e0dc5b5cf6.json
TemplateUriReadOnlySas: https://spfarmstaging.blob.core.windows.net/system/
Microsoft.Compute/Images/spfarmstaging/packer-vmTemplate.30ec65ab-39ed-
43a2-b6c4-62e0dc5b5cf6.json?se=2018-02-28T15%3A31%3A58Z&sig=94AD24%2F%2BsGX
ynOuBsEDzb%2FHljxogQAb972G21lt8z%2BE%3D&sp=r&sr=b&sv=2015-02-21
```

Now that we've created our Azure VM image using Packer, we have a VHD file stored in Azure in the storage account that we created via the Bash script earlier. It is ready to be used by our Terraform configuration. But first, we must set up Terraform remote state, which allows us to collaborate on IaC within a team setting, as the state is not stored locally.

Configuring the Terraform Remote State

Once we have the Azure CLI fully configured, we are ready to start working with Terraform. We must first set up storage and versioning of the Terraform state. Terraform state controls how changes to the infrastructure are tracked. In a team environment, this is a must-have for multiple team members making changes as part of the overall team workflow.

Note that the default Terraform state is stored on the local disk in the location where the Terraform command was run.

Tip   Terraform state contains sensitive data such as secrets which you do not want to expose publicly. Please refer to `www.terraform.io/docs/state/index.html` for more information.

There are several options when it comes to managing state for Terraform and setting up the back end. One option is to use the Terraform Enterprise product by HashiCorp. There are several others, including Consul, AWS, and S3.

The supported back end that we will use is AzureRM with versioning enabled.

Tip   To view a list of supported back ends, please visit `www.terraform.io/docs/backends/types/index.html`.

We create a file called `backend.tf` to hold the top level Terraform back-end configuration.

The Backend.tf File

To configure remote state, we add the following snippet to the `backend.tf` file within the `terraform/azure/environments/staging` folder, as follows.

Listing 4-2. The remote state resource configuration within the backend.tf file contents

```
terraform {
 backend "azurerm" {}
}
```

The `backend.tf` file will be checked into source control; therefore, we want to avoid putting sensitive information inside. To avoid doing this, we use another file called `beconf.tfvars`, which contains the sensitive information needed to initiate the back-end remote state (this is not checked into source control).

The contents of the `beconf.tfvars` should include the following key value pairs.

```
storage_account_name = "spfarmstagingacct"
container_name        = "spfarmstaging"
key                   = "staging-terraform-tfstate"
access_key            = "xxxx"
```

The values of the contents of the `beconf.tfvars` file come from the output of the Bash script that we ran successfully. With the exception of the `access_key` value, we must go to blob storage and obtain it manually via the Azure portal, under the Blob Storage settings.

In addition, you need to go to the Azure portal and create the container called `spfarmstaging` for the storage account, as the Bash script does not actually create that.

Please note that the value for `key` is the name of the Terraform state file that will be created in the storage container. Terraform automatically appends the `.tfstate` extension. In this case, the storage container is named `spfarmstaging`.

Warning   Ensure that you have obtained the access_key from the blob storage via the Azure portal prior to moving forward with Terraform init.

Run Terraform Init

Now that we configured our Azure remote state, we need to initialize Terraform for the Azure environment. Because we organized our Terraform folder by environment (AWS, local, Azure, etc.), we want to ensure we are within the `terraform/azure/environments/staging` folder prior to running the command. In this scenario, we are building a staging environment on Azure for our SharePoint 2016 farm.

Note   Terraform also has the concept of workspaces, but we do not use them for our exercise. You can learn more about workspaces at `www.terraform.io/docs/state/workspaces.html`.

With our `beconf.tfvars` file updated, we are now able to execute the command shown in Listing 4-3.

Listing 4-3. Successful Console Output from Running the Terraform init Command

```
>$ terraform init –backend-config=./beconf.tfvars

Initializing the backend...

Initializing provider plugins...

The following providers do not have any version constraints in
configuration, so the latest version was installed.

To prevent automatic upgrades to new major versions that may contain breaking
changes, it is recommended to add version = "..." constraints to the
corresponding provider blocks in configuration, with the constraint strings
suggested below.

* provider.azurerm: version = "~> 1.0"

Terraform has been successfully initialized!

You may now begin working with Terraform. Try running "terraform plan" to see
```

any changes that are required for your infrastructure. All Terraform commands should now work.

If you ever set or change modules or backend configuration for Terraform, rerun this command to reinitialize your working directory. If you forget, other commands will detect it and remind you to do so if necessary..

The output is quite helpful, actually. There are two takeaways from this output that we can spot. First, Terraform is downloading the AzureRM provider. As of Terraform v0.10, the providers have been decoupled for good reasons. One reason is version constraint for a given solution. The following is a blurb from the announcement by HashiCorp:

> *As of v0.10, provider plugins are no longer included in the main Terraform distribution. Instead, they are distributed separately and installed automatically by the terraform init command. In the long run, this new approach should be beneficial to anyone who wishes to upgrade a specific provider to get new functionality without also upgrading another provider that may have introduced incompatible changes. In the short term, it just means a smaller distribution package and thus avoiding the need to download tens of providers that may never be used.*

Second, we can constrain the AzureRM provider to a specific version moving forward. For us, this means going into our provider file located at `terraform/shared/providers/azure.tf`, and adding the suggested snippet of code. Our file should look like Listing 4-4.

Listing 4-4. Contents of the azure.tf Provider File Constraining the Version of the AzureRM Provider for Our Solution

```
provider.azurerm: version = "~> 1.0"
provider "azurerm" {
    subscription_id = "${var.subscription_id}"
    client_id = "${var.client_id}"
    client_secret = "${var.client_secret}"
    tenant_id =  "${var.tenant_id}"
}
```

Create Core Azure Resources Using Terraform

We have finally initialized our Azure environment, and our Terraform state is now stored in Azure. We are ready to start defining our SharePoint 2016 farm resources. Terraform uses HCL, or HashiCorp Configuration Language syntax. It looks similar to JSON, but unlike JSON, you can comment the document, and it is more readable by humans. Nonetheless, if you need to support JSON for the purpose of defining Terraform resources, you can do so because it acts the same way, irrespective of using HCL or JSON.

The first artifacts that we need to create (and this is typical) are the vNet, a security group, and any variables and output we would like to see at the time of running Terraform apply.

About Terraform Modules

Throughout this exercise, we use Terraform modules when declaring some resources, which are hosted on a separate repository. Think of modules as reusable components that can be used throughout your cloud environments. Modules may contain attributes that are populated via static text or dynamically via setting the corresponding variable's value. Module sources supported include local, HashiCorp Registry, GitHub, HTTP URLs, and S3 Buckets.

For our exercise, we want to keep our modules versioned on GitHub. They are located at `github.com/SharePointOscar/terraform_modules.git`. We will reference them directly from there. So, let's get started.

Note   Because the modules for Azure and AWS are on GitHub, you can opt to modify as you like by forking the repository. AWS and Azure resource specification continuously changes; therefore, we fully expect you might have to add or modify modules. Alternatively, you can opt not to use them and just use the Terraform built in resources directly.

Because we have our Terraform modules completely decoupled from our SharePoint 2016 Terraform project, we are able to modify the modules separately and even version them or apply releases.

This can prove to be very powerful as we might encounter a scenario where our SharePoint Terraform project depends on a specific release of the Azure vNet module. In such a case, we would want to specify the release within the module source.

Defining the Core Networking Resources

One of the first tasks is to define the core components in our virtual private cloud. There are interrelated components, which we will also cover shortly.

We must first define the core vNET, network security groups, subnets, firewall rules, and ports, as follows. These reside within the `terraform/azure/environments/staging/main.tf` file.

As per the architecture diagram in Figure 4-1, we define the appropriate vNet and subnets shown next.

```
# Create a virtual network
resource "azurerm_virtual_network" "spfarmstaging-vnet" {
  name                = "spfarm_staging_network"
  address_space       = ["10.10.0.0/16"]
  location            = "West US"
  resource_group_name = "${var.resource_group_name}"

}

module "subnet-public-a" {

  source             = "github.com/SharePointOscar/terraform_
                        modules.git//azure_modules//GatewaySubnet"
  sb_name            = "spfarm-subnet-public-a"
  rg_name            = "${var.resource_group_name}"
  vnet_name          = "${azurerm_virtual_network.spfarmstaging-
                        vnet.name}"
  sb_addr_prefix     = "10.10.1.0/24"

}
```

```
module "subnet-public-b" {

    source                      = "github.com/SharePointOscar/terraform_
                                  modules.git//azure_modules//GatewaySubnet"
    sb_name                     = "spfarm-subnet-public-b"
    rg_name                     = "${var.resource_group_name}"
    vnet_name                   = "${azurerm_virtual_network.spfarmstaging-
                                  vnet.name}"
    sb_addr_prefix              = "10.10.2.0/24"

}
# Create Network Security Group and rule for backend
resource "azurerm_network_security_group" "spfarm-security-group-backend" {
    name                = "spfarm-security-group-backend"
    location            = "West US"
    resource_group_name = "${var.resource_group_name}"

    # allow SSH connections
    security_rule {
        name                       = "SSH"
        priority                   = 1001
        direction                  = "Inbound"
        access                     = "Allow"
        protocol                   = "Tcp"
        source_port_range          = "*"
        destination_port_range     = "22"
        source_address_prefix      = "*"
        destination_address_prefix = "*"
    }

    # allow WinRM connections
    security_rule {
        name                       = "WinRM"
        priority                   = 1002
        direction                  = "Inbound"
        access                     = "Allow"
        protocol                   = "Tcp"
```

```
        source_port_range         = "*"
        destination_port_range    = "5985"
        source_address_prefix     = "*"
        destination_address_prefix = "*"
    }

    # allow RDP connections
    security_rule {
        name                      = "RDP"
        priority                  = 1003
        direction                 = "Inbound"
        access                    = "Allow"
        protocol                  = "Tcp"
        source_port_range         = "*"
        destination_port_range    = "3389"
        source_address_prefix     = "*"
        destination_address_prefix = "*"
    }

  tags {
      environment = "Terraform Demo"
  }
}
# Create Network Security Group and rule
resource "azurerm_network_security_group" "spfarm-security-group-frontend" {
    name                = "spfarm-security-group-frontend"
    location            = "West US"
    resource_group_name = "${var.resource_group_name}"

    # allow SSH connections
    security_rule {
        name                      = "SSH"
        priority                  = 1001
        direction                 = "Inbound"
        access                    = "Allow"
        protocol                  = "Tcp"
        source_port_range         = "*"
```

```
            destination_port_range      = "22"
            source_address_prefix       = "*"
            destination_address_prefix = "*"
        }

        # allow WinRM connections
        security_rule {
            name                        = "WinRM"
            priority                    = 1002
            direction                   = "Inbound"
            access                      = "Allow"
            protocol                    = "Tcp"
            source_port_range           = "*"
            destination_port_range      = "5985"
            source_address_prefix       = "*"
            destination_address_prefix = "*"
        }

        # allow RDP connections
        security_rule {
            name                        = "RDP"
            priority                    = 1003
            direction                   = "Inbound"
            access                      = "Allow"
            protocol                    = "Tcp"
            source_port_range           = "*"
            destination_port_range      = "3389"
            source_address_prefix       = "*"
            destination_address_prefix = "*"
        }

    tags {
        environment = "Terraform Demo"
    }
}
```

```
// # DB1 Network settings
 resource "azurerm_public_ip" "db1-public-ip" {
  name                         = "db1-public-ip"
  location                     = "West US"
  resource_group_name          = "${var.resource_group_name}"
  public_ip_address_allocation = "static"

  tags {
    environment = "staging"
  }
}
resource "azurerm_network_interface" "spfarm-db1" {
  name                       = "network-interface-spfarm-db1"
  location                   = "West US"
  resource_group_name        = "${var.resource_group_name}"
  network_security_group_id  = "${azurerm_network_security_group.spfarm-
                                  security-group-backend.id}"
  dns_servers                = ["10.10.2.19"]

  ip_configuration {
    name                          = "db1-ipconfiguration"
    subnet_id                     = "${module.subnet-public-b.id}"
    public_ip_address_id          = "${azurerm_public_ip.db1-public-ip.id}"
    private_ip_address_allocation = "static"
    private_ip_address            = "10.10.2.17"
  }

  tags {
    environment = "Staging"
  }
}

resource "azurerm_public_ip" "appserver1-public-ip" {
  name                         = "appserver1-public-ip"
  location                     = "West US"
  resource_group_name          = "${var.resource_group_name}"
  public_ip_address_allocation = "static"
```

```
  tags {
    environment = "SharePoint 2016 Staging"
  }
}
resource "azurerm_network_interface" "spfarm-appserver1" {
  name                      = "network-interface-spfarm-appserver1"
  location                  = "West US"
  resource_group_name       = "${var.resource_group_name}"
  network_security_group_id = "${azurerm_network_security_group.spfarm-
                              security-group-backend.id}"
  dns_servers               = ["10.10.2.19"]

  ip_configuration {
    name                          = "appserver1-ipconfiguration"
    subnet_id                     = "${module.subnet-public-a.id}"
    public_ip_address_id          = "${azurerm_public_ip.appserver1-public-
                                    ip.id}"
    private_ip_address_allocation = "static"
    private_ip_address            = "10.10.1.18"

  }

  tags {
    environment = "SharePoint 2016 Staging"
  }
}
# WFE1 Network settings
resource "azurerm_public_ip" "wfe1-public-ip" {
  name                      = "wfe1-public-ip"
  location                  = "West US"
  resource_group_name       = "${var.resource_group_name}"
  public_ip_address_allocation = "static"
```

```
  tags {
    environment = "SharePoint 2016 Staging"
  }
}

resource "azurerm_network_interface" "spfarm-wfe1" {
  name                      = "network-interface-spfarm-wfe1"
  location                  = "West US"
  resource_group_name       = "${var.resource_group_name}"
  network_security_group_id = "${azurerm_network_security_group.spfarm-
                               security-group-frontend.id}"
  dns_servers               = ["10.10.2.19"]

  ip_configuration {
    name                          = "wfe1-ipconfiguration"
    subnet_id                     = "${module.subnet-public-a.id}"
    public_ip_address_id          = "${azurerm_public_ip.wfe1-public-ip.
                                     id}"
    private_ip_address_allocation = "static"
    private_ip_address            = "10.10.1.16"
  }

   tags {
    environment = "Staging"
  }
}

# AD1 Network settings
resource "azurerm_public_ip" "ad1-public-ip" {
  name                          = "ad1-public-ip"
  location                      = "West US"
  resource_group_name           = "${var.resource_group_name}"
  public_ip_address_allocation  = "static"

  tags {
    environment = "SharePoint 2016 Staging"
  }
}
```

```
resource "azurerm_network_interface" "spfarm-ad1" {
  name                    = "network-interface-spfarm-ad1"
  location                = "West US"
  resource_group_name = "${var.resource_group_name}"
  network_security_group_id = "${azurerm_network_security_group.spfarm-
                                 security-group-backend.id}"

  ip_configuration {
    name                           = "AD1-ipconfiguration"
    subnet_id                      = "${module.subnet-public-b.id}"
    public_ip_address_id           = "${azurerm_public_ip.ad1-public-ip.id}"
    private_ip_address_allocation  = "static"
    private_ip_address             = "10.10.2.19"
  }

  tags {
    environment = "SharePoint 2016 Staging"
  }
}
```

Many foundational resources have been declared including two security groups: one for back-end resources and one for front-end resources. We also defined two subnets, which are attached to their corresponding subnet and network security group. Had we not used Terraform modules, we would have repeated ourselves quite a bit in terms of declaring the same resources over and over again. Maintaining this code would prove to be an onerous task as our project grows.

To ensure we get the modules registered within our solution, we must execute the `terraform get` command.

```
> $ terraform get
- module.subnet-public-a
- module.subnet-public-b
```

Because we've only used two Azure modules thus far, that is exactly what we get from the output of our command.

Tip   if you wish to refresh all modules, execute `terraform get -update=true` and all modules will be downloaded.

After defining our core network resources in Azure, we are ready to define our virtual machines in our SharePoint 2016 farm topology.

Terraforming the SharePoint 2016 Servers in the Farm Topology

The next Azure resources we need to define are the different virtual machines that are part of our SharePoint 2016 farm topology. Recall in Chapter 3, our topology included several server roles. We will define these same roles in Terraform to deploy them to AWS. We later use Ansible to perform configuration management, and install and configure the SharePoint 2016 domain controller and join all VMs to the newly configured domain.

The following are the roles that we will define via Terraform:

- Domain controller

- Database server

- Application server

- Web front end

Note   If you recall, earlier in this chapter, we used Packer to create our "golden image." This is the Azure VM image we use throughout our Terraform project to create Azure VMs corresponding to the SharePoint server roles within the farm. However, we do *not* use our custom Azure VM for SQL because we want to leverage the one available in the gallery that contains the preinstalled SQL software.

Preparing to Deploy Resources to Azure

Now that we have all of our AWS SharePoint farm resources declared, it is time to deploy the resources. To do this, we first want to ensure that our configuration is validated by executing terraform validate.

```
> $ terraform validate
```

You should not see any errors at this point. If that is the case, then you want to proceed to execute a Terraform plan to ensure that all of your resources will be created as expected.

Execute Terraform Plan

It is a good practice to also execute the plan command to ensure that all looks good. But most importantly, you can verify the proposed creation or modification of resources, is what is expected. In addition, it is a great way to capture changes that may or may not need to be executed right away.

The `terraform plan` command accepts several optional parameters (you can type `terraform plan -h` to obtain a full list). Of special interest, is the `-out=path` because it allows you to specify a file where you save the planned deployment. This file can then be used as input for executing the `terraform apply` command later.

```
>$ terraform plan –out=./azure_spfarm_staging.plan –var-file=./terraform.
tfvars
```

This outputs a long list of resources with values for some attributes, and others show `<computed>`, which are computed at runtime when you execute the `terraform apply` command. The following is a trimmed down look at our output showing the WFE configuration.

```
Refreshing Terraform state in-memory prior to plan...
The refreshed state will be used to calculate this plan, but will not be
persisted to local or remote state storage.

------------------------------------------------------------------------

An execution plan has been generated and is shown below.
Resource actions are indicated with the following symbols:
  + create

Terraform will perform the following actions:

  ...trimmed for brevity...

  + azurerm_public_ip.ad1-public-ip
      id:                                          <computed>
      fqdn:                                        <computed>
      ip_address:                                  <computed>
```

116

```
    location:                              "westus"
    name:                                  "ad1-public-ip"
    public_ip_address_allocation:          "static"
    resource_group_name:                   "spfarmstaging"
    sku:                                   "Basic"
    tags.%:                                "1"
    tags.environment:                      "SharePoint 2016
                                           Staging"

+ azurerm_public_ip.appserver1-public-ip
    id:                                    <computed>
    fqdn:                                  <computed>
    ip_address:                            <computed>
    location:                              "westus"
    name:                                  "appserver1-public-ip"
    public_ip_address_allocation:          "static"
    resource_group_name:                   "spfarmstaging"
    sku:                                   "Basic"
    tags.%:                                "1"
    tags.environment:                      "SharePoint 2016
                                           Staging"

+ azurerm_public_ip.db1-public-ip
    id:                                    <computed>
    fqdn:                                  <computed>
    ip_address:                            <computed>
    location:                              "westus"
    name:                                  "db1-public-ip"
    public_ip_address_allocation:          "static"
    resource_group_name:                   "spfarmstaging"
    sku:                                   "Basic"
    tags.%:                                "1"
    tags.environment:                      "staging"

+ azurerm_public_ip.webfrontend-lb-public-ip
    id:                                    <computed>
    fqdn:                                  <computed>
```

```
          ip_address:                        <computed>
          location:                          "westus"
          name:                              "webfrontend-lb-
                                             public-ip"

          public_ip_address_allocation:      "static"
          resource_group_name:               "spfarmstaging"
          sku:                               "Basic"
          tags.%:                            "1"
          tags.environment:                  "SharePoint 2016
                                             Staging"


  + azurerm_public_ip.wfe-public-ip[0]
          id:                                <computed>
          fqdn:                              <computed>
          ip_address:                        <computed>
          location:                          "westus"
          name:                              "wfe0-public-ip"
          public_ip_address_allocation:      "static"
          resource_group_name:               "spfarmstaging"
          sku:                               "Basic"
          tags.%:                            "1"
          tags.environment:                  "SharePoint 2016
                                             Staging"


  + azurerm_public_ip.wfe-public-ip[1]
          id:                                <computed>
          fqdn:                              <computed>
          ip_address:                        <computed>
          location:                          "westus"
          name:                              "wfe1-public-ip"
          public_ip_address_allocation:      "static"
          resource_group_name:               "spfarmstaging"
          sku:                               "Basic"
          tags.%:                            "1"
          tags.environment:                  "SharePoint 2016
                                             Staging"
```

```
+ azurerm_subnet.subnet-frontend
    id:                                          <computed>
    address_prefix:                              "10.10.3.0/24"
    ip_configurations.#:                         <computed>
    name:                                        "spfarm-subnet-
                                                 frontend"
    resource_group_name:                         "spfarmstaging"
    virtual_network_name:                        "spfarm_staging_
                                                 network"

...

+ azurerm_virtual_machine.spfarm_wfe1
    id:                                          <computed>
    availability_set_id:                         "${azurerm_
                                                 availability_set.
                                                 webfrontend_
                                                 availabilityset.id}"

    delete_data_disks_on_termination:           "true"
    delete_os_disk_on_termination:              "false"
    identity.#:                                  <computed>
    location:                                    "westus"
    name:                                        "SP2016WFE"
    network_interface_ids.#:                     <computed>
    os_profile.#:                                "1"
    os_profile.1539969592.admin_password:        <sensitive>
    os_profile.1539969592.admin_username:        "packer"
    os_profile.1539969592.computer_name:         "SP2016WFE0"
    os_profile.1539969592.custom_data:           <computed>
    os_profile_windows_config.#:                 "1"
    os_profile_windows_config.2256145325.additional_
    unattend_config.#:                           "0"
    os_profile_windows_config.2256145325.enable_
    automatic_upgrades:                          "true"
    os_profile_windows_config.2256145325.provision_
    vm_agent:                                    "true"
    os_profile_windows_config.2256145325.winrm.#: "0"
    resource_group_name:                         "spfarmstaging"
```

119

```
        storage_image_reference.#:              <computed>
        storage_os_disk.#:                      "1"
        storage_os_disk.0.caching:              "ReadWrite"
        storage_os_disk.0.create_option:        "FromImage"
        storage_os_disk.0.disk_size_gb:         <computed>
        storage_os_disk.0.image_uri:            "https://spfarms
                                                taging.blob.
                                                core.windows.net/
                                                system/Microsoft.
                                                Compute/Images/
                                                spfarmstaging/packer-
                                                osDisk.5fd747c3-
                                                2933-4f09-af1e-
                                                12bf65d1c476.vhd"
        storage_os_disk.0.managed_disk_id:      <computed>
        storage_os_disk.0.managed_disk_type:    <computed>
        storage_os_disk.0.name:                 "WFE0-osdisk1"
        storage_os_disk.0.os_type:              "Windows"
        storage_os_disk.0.vhd_uri:              "https://spfarm
                                                staging.blob.
                                                core.windows.net/
                                                spfarmstaging/wfe0-
                                                osdisk.vhd"
        tags.%:                                 <computed>
        vm_size:                                "Standard_DS2_v2"

 + azurerm_virtual_network.spfarmstaging-vnet
        id:                                     <computed>
        address_space.#:                        "2"
        address_space.0:                        "10.10.0.0/16"
        address_space.1:                        "10.10.0.0/16"
        location:                               "westus"
        name:                                   "spfarm_staging_
                                                network"
        resource_group_name:                    "spfarmstaging"
        subnet.#:                               <computed>
        tags.%:                                 <computed>
```

```
+ module.subnet-application.azurerm_subnet.main
    id:                                       <computed>
    address_prefix:                           "10.10.2.0/24"
    ip_configurations.#:                      <computed>
    name:                                     "spfarm-subnet-
                                              application"

    resource_group_name:                      "spfarmstaging"
    virtual_network_name:                     "spfarm_staging_
                                              network"


+ module.subnet-backend.azurerm_subnet.main
    id:                                       <computed>
    address_prefix:                           "10.10.1.0/24"
    ip_configurations.#:                      <computed>
    name:                                     "spfarm-subnet-backend"
    resource_group_name:                       "spfarmstaging"
    virtual_network_name:                     "spfarm_staging_network"

Plan: 30 to add, 0 to change, 0 to destroy.

-----------------------------------------------------------------------

This plan was saved to: azure_spfarm_staging.plan

To perform exactly these actions, run the following command to apply:
    terraform apply " azure_spfarm_staging.plan"
```

Executing Terraform Apply

We've executed the `terraform plan` command and saved the proposed plan to a file. We like what we see and wish to now deploy all the related resources to Azure. We do this by executing the command shown in Listing 4-5.

Listing 4-5. A Partial View of the output When Executing the terraform plan Command

```
$ terraform apply azure_spfarm_staging.plan

Refreshing Terraform state in-memory prior to plan...
The refreshed state will be used to calculate this plan, but will not be
```

persisted to local or remote state storage.

An execution plan has been generated and is shown below.
Resource actions are indicated with the following symbols:
  + create

Terraform will perform the following actions:

```
  + azurerm_network_interface.spfarm-ad1
      id:                                            <computed>
      applied_dns_servers.#:                         <computed>
      dns_servers.#:                                 <computed>
      enable_accelerated_networking:                 "false"
      enable_ip_forwarding:                          "false"
      internal_dns_name_label:                       <computed>
      internal_fqdn:                                 <computed>
      ip_configuration.#:                            "1"
      ip_configuration.0.load_balancer_backend_
      address_pools_ids.#:                           <computed>
      ip_configuration.0.load_balancer_
      inbound_nat_rules_ids.#:                       <computed>
      ip_configuration.0.name:                       "db1-ipconfiguration"
      ip_configuration.0.primary:                    <computed>
      ip_configuration.0.private_ip_address:         <computed>
      ip_configuration.0.private_ip_address_
      allocation:                                    "dynamic"
      ip_configuration.0.public_ip_address_id:       "${azurerm_public_
                                                     ip.ad1-public-ip.id}"

      ip_configuration.0.subnet_id:                  "${module.subnet-
                                                     public-a.id}"

      location:                                      "westus"
      mac_address:                                   <computed>
      name:                                          "network-interface-
                                                     spfarm-ad1"

      network_security_group_id:                     "${azurerm_network_
                                                     security_group.spfarm-
                                                     security-group.id}"
```

122

```
      private_ip_address:                          <computed>
      private_ip_addresses.#:                      <computed>
      resource_group_name:                         "spfarmstaging"
      tags.%:                                      "1"
      tags.environment:                            "staging"
      virtual_machine_id:                          <computed>

..

+ azurerm_network_interface.spfarm-db1
      id:                                          <computed>
      applied_dns_servers.#:                       <computed>
      dns_servers.#:                               <computed>
      enable_accelerated_networking:               "false"
      enable_ip_forwarding:                        "false"
      internal_dns_name_label:                     <computed>
      internal_fqdn:                               <computed>
      ip_configuration.#:                          "1"
      ip_configuration.0.load_balancer_backend_
      address_pools_ids.#:                         <computed>
      ip_configuration.0.load_balancer_inbound_
      nat_rules_ids.#:                             <computed>
      ip_configuration.0.name:                     "db1-ipconfiguration"
      ip_configuration.0.primary:                  <computed>
      ip_configuration.0.private_ip_address:       <computed>
      ip_configuration.0.private_ip_address_
      allocation:                                  "dynamic"
      ip_configuration.0.public_ip_address_id:     "${azurerm_public_
                                                   ip.db1-public-ip.id}"

      ip_configuration.0.subnet_id:                "${module.subnet-
                                                   public-a.id}"

      location:                                    "westus"
      mac_address:                                 <computed>
      name:                                        "network-interface-
                                                   spfarm-db1"
```

```
    network_security_group_id:              "${azurerm_network_
                                            security_group.spfarm-
                                            security-group.id}"

    private_ip_address:                     <computed>
    private_ip_addresses.#:                 <computed>
    resource_group_name:                    "spfarmstaging"
    tags.%:                                 "1"
    tags.environment:                       "staging"
    virtual_machine_id:                     <computed>

+ azurerm_network_interface.spfarm-wfe1
    id:                                     <computed>
    applied_dns_servers.#:                  <computed>
    dns_servers.#:                          <computed>
    enable_accelerated_networking:          "false"
    enable_ip_forwarding:                   "false"
    internal_dns_name_label:                <computed>
    internal_fqdn:                          <computed>
    ip_configuration.#:                     "1"
    ip_configuration.0.load_balancer_backend_
    address_pools_ids.#:                    <computed>
    ip_configuration.0.load_balancer_inbound_
    nat_rules_ids.#:                        <computed>
    ip_configuration.0.name:                "wfe1-ipconfiguration"
    ip_configuration.0.primary:             <computed>
    ip_configuration.0.private_ip_address:  <computed>
    ip_configuration.0.private_ip_address_
    allocation:                             "dynamic"
    ip_configuration.0.public_ip_address_id:  "${azurerm_public_
                                            ip.wfe1-public-ip.id}"

    ip_configuration.0.subnet_id:           "${module.subnet-
                                            public-a.id}"

    location:                               "westus"
    mac_address:                            <computed>
    name:                                   "network-interface-
                                            spfarm-wfe1"
```

```
    network_security_group_id:                      "${azurerm_network_
                                                     security_group.spfarm-
                                                     security-group.id}"

    private_ip_address:                             <computed>
    private_ip_addresses.#:                         <computed>
    resource_group_name:                            "spfarmstaging"
    tags.%:                                          "1"
    tags.environment:                               "staging"
    virtual_machine_id:                             <computed>

+ azurerm_network_security_group.spfarm-security-group
    id:                                             <computed>
    location:                                       "westus"
    name:                                           "spfarm-security-group"
    resource_group_name:                            "spfarmstaging"
    security_rule.#:                                "3"
    security_rule.0.access:                         "Allow"
    security_rule.0.destination_address_prefix:     "*"
    security_rule.0.destination_port_range:         "22"
    security_rule.0.direction:                      "Inbound"
    security_rule.0.name:                           "SSH"
    security_rule.0.priority:                       "1001"
    security_rule.0.protocol:                       "tcp"
    security_rule.0.source_address_prefix:          "*"
    security_rule.0.source_port_range:              "*"
    security_rule.1.access:                         "Allow"
    security_rule.1.destination_address_prefix:     "*"
    security_rule.1.destination_port_range:         "5985"
    security_rule.1.direction:                      "Inbound"
    security_rule.1.name:                           "WinRM"
    security_rule.1.priority:                       "1002"
    security_rule.1.protocol:                       "tcp"
    security_rule.1.source_address_prefix:          "*"
    security_rule.1.source_port_range:              "*"
    security_rule.2.access:                         "Allow"
```

```
        security_rule.2.destination_address_prefix:    "*"
        security_rule.2.destination_port_range:        "3389"
        security_rule.2.direction:                     "Inbound"
        security_rule.2.name:                          "RDP"
        security_rule.2.priority:                      "1003"
        security_rule.2.protocol:                      "tcp"
        security_rule.2.source_address_prefix:         "*"
        security_rule.2.source_port_range:             "*"
        tags.%:                                        "1"
        tags.environment:                              "Staging"

  + azurerm_public_ip.ad1-public-ip
        id:                                            <computed>
        fqdn:                                          <computed>
        ip_address:                                    <computed>
        location:                                      "westus"
        name:                                          "ad1-public-ip"
        public_ip_address_allocation:                  "static"
        resource_group_name:                           "spfarmstaging"
        tags.%:                                        "1"
        tags.environment:                              "staging"

  + azurerm_public_ip.appserver1-public-ip
        id:                                            <computed>
        fqdn:                                          <computed>
        ip_address:                                    <computed>
        location:                                      "westus"
        name:                                          "appserver1-public-ip"
        public_ip_address_allocation:                  "static"
        resource_group_name:                           "spfarmstaging"
        tags.%:                                        "1"
        tags.environment:                              "staging"

  + azurerm_public_ip.db1-public-ip
        id:                                            <computed>
        fqdn:                                          <computed>
        ip_address:                                    <computed>
```

```
        location:                              "westus"
        name:                                  "db1-public-ip"
        public_ip_address_allocation:          "static"
        resource_group_name:                   "spfarmstaging"
        tags.%:                                "1"
        tags.environment:                      "staging"

+ azurerm_public_ip.wfe1-public-ip
        id:                                    <computed>
        fqdn:                                  <computed>
        ip_address:                            <computed>
        location:                              "westus"
        name:                                  "wfe1-public-ip"
        public_ip_address_allocation:          "static"
        resource_group_name:                   "spfarmstaging"
        tags.%:                                "1"
        tags.environment:                      "staging"

...

+ azurerm_virtual_network.network
        id:                                    <computed>
        address_space.#:                       "1"
        address_space.0:                       "10.10.0.0/16"
        location:                              "westus"
        name:                                  "spfarm_staging_network"
        resource_group_name:                   "spfarmstaging"
        subnet.#:                              <computed>
        tags.%:                                <computed>

+ module.subnet-public-a.azurerm_subnet.main
        id:                                    <computed>
        address_prefix:                        "10.10.1.0/24"
        ip_configurations.#:                   <computed>
        name:                                  "spfarm-subnet-public-a"
        resource_group_name:                   "spfarmstaging"
        virtual_network_name:                  "spfarm_staging_network"
```

```
+ module.subnet-public-b.azurerm_subnet.main
    id:                              <computed>
    address_prefix:                  "10.10.2.0/24"
    ip_configurations.#:             <computed>
    name:                            "spfarm-subnet-
                                     public-b"

    resource_group_name:             "spfarmstaging"
    virtual_network_name:            "spfarm_staging_
                                     network"
```

```
Plan: 16 to add, 0 to change, 0 to destroy.
```

```
This plan was saved to: azure_spfarm_staging_plan.plan
```

```
To perform exactly these actions, run the following command to apply:
    terraform apply "azure_spfarm_staging_plan.plan"
```

The output is quite lengthy, so we won't show you this. However, you can also use the following command.

```
>$ terraform show
```

At this point, you should see all the resources created by visiting the Azure portal.

Caution   You may incur charges deploying resources to Azure. It is recommended that you destroy the resources as soon as possible to avoid charges.

We've gone through the process of deploying our entire SharePoint infrastructure to Azure, but we are not done yet! We need to ensure that our infrastructure is configured as desired. Since we are using IaC, we can apply the development principles, including writing test cases.

Fortunately for us, we have InSpec 2.0. InSpec is a framework that helps test configuration and as of 2.0, cloud resource configuration. It is widely used in automation scenarios such as ours.

Testing Terraform Infrastructure Deployments Using InSpec

When we built our development SharePoint 2016 farm in Chapter 3, we included a way to test and confirm that our configuration was in the desired state by using Serverspec.

Because we are writing infrastructure as code, it is quite appropriate to also write tests to ensure that our end result is what we expect it to be. Testing Terraform deployed resources in AWS and Azure has become easier thanks to the newest version of InSpec 2.0, which brings this capability.

About InSpec 2.0

InSpec is an automated testing framework, which allows you to write unit tests against a Windows configuration (for example) to validate that specific Windows features are enabled. As of InSpec 2.0, however, we can now test specific cloud provider resources, such as AWS and Azure resources that have been deployed with Terraform.

The unit tests we write can be incorporated into a CI/CD pipeline using Jenkins or VSTS. InSpec is effectively Compliance as Code (CaC), which until now was a missing piece when provisioning IaC. You can learn more about open source InSpec at www.inspec.io.

Getting Started

Our infrastructure tests reside within the `terraform/tests/azure` folder. This folder was created using the `inspec init profile terraform/tests/azure` command, which creates a file structure needed to start creating tests against our infrastructure.

We need to ensure that the Azure environment variables are set prior to executing tests. This is because InSpec uses the Azure API to run the tests against the terraformed Azure resources.

To set the environment variables on your terminal, simply fill in the required information and paste the following snippet.

```
>$ export AZURE_CLIENT_ID='55555555-7844-40c9-bdd4-6ba2868d9121' \
export AZURE_SECRET='pass@word1!' \
export AZURE_SUBSCRIPTION_ID='dbbc2e47-bae1-5555-a35a-35a7adc3e293' \
export AZURE_TENANT='484c7f71-4542-5555-8e1a-87e4751f4750'
```

Terraform Output

InSpec 2.0 leverages the Terraform output defined. This is needed to write meaningful test cases, as we use the actual existing values of various resources to write our tests. To have a readable file for InSpec, we export the Terraform output by executing the following command within the `terraform/azure/environments/staging` folder location.

```
>$ terraform output --json > ../../../tests/azure/files/terraform.json
```

The command places the `terraform.json` file in the appropriate location for the test scripts to find it.

Armed with the values of these variables, we are ready to start writing some test cases. There are particular things we care about when deploying our SharePoint farm topology to Azure.

Testing Our Resource Group

We would like to run some tests on our resource group, which we named spfarmstaging, in our Terraform configuration file. We want to verify the following:

- The number of virtual machines that our resource group contains. If you recall, our SharePoint 2016 farm topology has a total of four virtual machines.

- Since there are four virtual machines, each one has at least one network interface (nic). We are expecting four.

- The name of our resource group is as we specified.

- The location of our resource group should be in westus.

- We have created two NSGs to protect their corresponding subnets (the back-end and front-end subnets).

We created a test file at the following location on our GitHub repo `terraform/tests/ azure/controls/resource_group.rb`. and its contents are shown in Listing 4-6.

Listing 4-6. Contents of the resource_group.rb Infrastructure Test File

```
control 'azure_spfarm_storage' do
    title 'Verify the SharePoint 2016 Farm Azure primary Resource Group
    configuration.'
```

```
  impact 1.0

describe azure_resource_group(name: 'spfarmstaging') do

  # Check if the number of VMs in the Resource Group is correct
  (for SharePoint 2016 topology we have 4)
  its('vm_count') { should eq 4 }

  # Check if the number of public IPs is correct, should be 4 one for
  each VM
  its('public_ip_count') { should eq 4 }

  its('name') { should eq 'spfarmstaging' }

  #storage should be in the West US
  its('location') { should cmp 'westus' }

  # We have two NSGs for our solution
  its('nsg_count') { should eq 2 }

  end
end
```

Testing Virtual Machines

Virtual machines are another set of resources deployed via Terraform. For our virtual machines, we have a few critical things we want to test, which include the following tests.

- Our virtual machine should be located in the 'westus'

- Our virtual machine should contain network interfaces

- The total network interace count should be one

- The size of our virtual machine should be Standard_DS2_v2

- Our virtual machine should have resource tags (we can also check for a specific tag)

Our test file is located at terraform/tests/azure/controls/virtual_machines.rb. We used only test two machines to give you a sense of what is possible, however.

```
control 'azure_spfarm_virtual_machines' do
  title 'Verify the SharePoint 2016 Farm Virtual Machines are configured as
  required.'
  impact 1.0

  describe azure_virtual_machine(group_name: 'spfarmstaging', name:
'sp2016AppServer') do

    # Check if the VM is located in the correct region
    its('location') { should cmp 'westus' }

     # should have nics attached to it
    it { should have_nics }

    # The Public Address Network Interface should exist
    its('nic_count') {should eq 1}

    # Check if the VM has the correct size
    its('vm_size') { should cmp 'Standard_DS2_v2' }

    # Check if the VM has tags
    it { should have_tags }
  end

  describe azure_virtual_machine(group_name: 'spfarmstaging', name:
'SP2016SQLSERVER') do

    # Check if the VM is located in the correct region
    its('location') { should cmp 'westus' }

    # should have nics attached to it
    it { should have_nics }

    # The Public Address Network Interface should exist
    its('nic_count') {should eq 1}

    # Check if the VM has the correct image
    its('publisher') { should cmp 'MicrosoftSQLServer' }
    its('offer') { should cmp 'SQL2014SP2-WS2012R2' }
    its('sku') { should cmp 'Enterprise' }
```

```
  # Check if the VM has the correct size
  its('vm_size') { should cmp 'Standard_DS2_v2' }

  # Check if the VM has the correct admin username
  its('admin_username') { should eq 'packer' }

  # Check if the VM has tags, as per business requirements
  it { should have_tags }
  end
end
```

Executing InSpec Tests

Now that we've written our test cases against our Azure resources, we are ready to execute our test suite by using the following command.

```
>$ inspec exec test/azure -t azure://
```

The output may look familiar if you've used other testing frameworks, which is shown in Listing 4-7.

Listing 4-7. A Successful InSpec Test Execution

```
Profile: InSpec Profile (Test Azure Resources Deployed via Terraform)
Version: 0.1.0
Target:  azure://88888888-bae1-4b8b-a35a-35a7adc3e293

  ✓  check-securityRules: azure_generic_resource
    ✓  azure_generic_resource name should cmp == "spfarm-security-group-
       backend"
    ✓  azure_generic_resource location should cmp == "westus"
    ✓  azure_generic_resource properties.securityRules.count should eq 3
  ✓  azure_spfarm_storage: Verify the SharePoint 2016 Farm Azure primary
     Resource Group configuration.
    ✓  azure_resource_group vm_count should eq 4
    ✓  azure_resource_group public_ip_count should eq 4
    ✓  azure_resource_group name should eq "spfarmstaging"
    ✓  azure_resource_group location should cmp == "westus"
    ✓  azure_resource_group nsg_count should eq 2
```

✓ `azure_spfarm_virtual_machines`: Verify the SharePoint 2016 Farm
   Virtual Machines are configured as required.

    ✓ `azure_virtual_machine should have nics`
    ✓ `azure_virtual_machine location should cmp == "westus"`
    ✓ `azure_virtual_machine nic_count should eq 1`
    ✓ `azure_virtual_machine vm_size should cmp == "Standard_DS2_v2"`
    ✓ `azure_virtual_machine should have nics`
    ✓ `azure_virtual_machine location should cmp == "westus"`
    ✓ `azure_virtual_machine nic_count should eq 1`
    ✓ `azure_virtual_machine publisher should cmp == "MicrosoftSQLServer"`
    ✓ `azure_virtual_machine offer should cmp == "SQL2014SP2-WS2012R2"`
    ✓ `azure_virtual_machine sku should cmp == "Enterprise"`
    ✓ `azure_virtual_machine vm_size should cmp == "Standard_DS2_v2"`
    ✓ `azure_virtual_machine admin_username should eq "packer"`

```
Profile Summary: 3 successful controls, 0 control failures, 0 controls
skipped
Test Summary: 20 successful, 0 failures, 0 skipped
```

We need to now perform configuration management tasks using Ansible. These are the same playbooks we executed when building the Vagrant test environment for SharePoint in Chapter 3. Before that, we must ensure that Ansible has an inventory of the Azure VMs, including the IP addresses. In our next section, we cover how to generate an Ansible dynamic inventory from Azure resources.

Generating the Dynamic Ansible Inventory File for Azure Resources

Because we are using Azure virtual machine resources, we expect that at any given point, we can tear down and re-create the virtual machines, which means IP addresses will change. Therefore, instead of having a static Ansible inventory file, as we had for our Vagrant SharePoint test environment, we want to build it based on the existing virtual machines deployed to Azure.

Using azure_rm.py and azure_rm.ini Files Provided by Ansible

We could figure out how to build a dynamic inventory file for Ansible from scratch. But there is no need to do so, given that Ansible provides a Python script for us to use (see `https://github.com/ansible/ansible/blob/devel/contrib/inventory`).

Tip   Ansible now supports "inventory plugins" which enhance the capabilities of dynamic inventory scripts by providing access to Ansible's internals. At the time of writing this book, there isn't an inventory plug-in for Azure, but check at `https://docs.ansible.com/ansible/latest/plugins/inventory.html`, as it is potentially included in the upcoming Ansible 2.7 release.

First, download the two files into the project's `ansible` folder and ensure that the `azure_rm.py` file is executable by using `chmod u+x azure_rm.py`.

`azure_rm.in` serves as a configuration file and can be customized; for example, we may not be using some of the services listed, which can be commented out. In addition, we can constrain our calls to focus on querying a specific resource group. In our case, we have modified the file to only query the `spfarmstaging` Azure resource group and only from the `westus` location, as shown in Listing 4-8.

Listing 4-8.   Contents of the azure_rm.ini File Customized to Only Show Westus Resources from the Spfarmstaging Resource Group

```
# Configuration file for azure_rm.py
#
[azure]
# Control which resource groups are included. By default all resources
groups are included.
# Set resource_groups to a comma separated list of resource groups names.
resource_groups=spfarmstaging

# Control which tags are included. Set tags to a comma separated list of
keys or key:value pairs
#tags=
```

```
# Control which locations are included. Set locations to a comma separated
list (e.g. eastus,eastus2,westus)
locations=westus

# Include powerstate. If you don't need powerstate information, turning it
off improves runtime performance.
include_powerstate=yes

# Control grouping with the following boolean flags. Valid values: yes, no,
true, false, True, False, 0, 1.
group_by_resource_group=yes
group_by_location=yes
group_by_security_group=yes
group_by_tag=yes
```

Installing Azure Python SDK

Ansible requires additional packages in order to work with Azure. To install these, we use pip (Python package manager) and execute the following command.

```
>$ pip install ansible[azure]
```

This installs all required packages. We list those using grep to filter the results. It should look something like the following.

```
> $ pip list | grep azure
DEPRECATION: The default format will switch to columns in the future. You
can use --format=(legacy|columns) (or define a format=(legacy|columns) in
your pip.conf under the [list] section) to disable this warning.
azure-cli-nspkg (3.0.1)
azure-common (1.1.8)
azure-mgmt-compute (2.1.0)
azure-mgmt-network (1.7.1)
azure-mgmt-nspkg (2.0.0)
azure-mgmt-resource (1.2.2)
azure-mgmt-storage (1.5.0)
azure-nspkg (2.0.0)
azure-storage (0.35.1)
msrestazure (0.4.21)
```

Tip   If you get permission denied errors, you might need to adjust the command and use sudo (i.e., sudo pip install ansible[azure]).

Configuring Ansible Credentials Using Environment Variables

To use the provided Python script, we need to ensure that we have certain environment variables set. These environment variables can be created from the output of our Bash script mentioned in the "Create Base VM Image Using Packer" section. You can also grab the values from the packer/azure_windows_2016.json file, as it uses these values. On our terminal, we set the following environment variables.

```
>$ export AZURE_CLIENT_ID='<REDACTED>' \
export AZURE_SECRET='pass@word1' \
export AZURE_SUBSCRIPTION_ID='<REDACTED>' \
export AZURE_TENANT='<REDACTED>
```

Warning   You must set the environment variables successfully before moving on because the Ansible Python script will not be able to authenticate to Azure otherwise. Recall that we obtained that information from running our Bash script earlier in this chapter, and can use this information to set these environment variables when using Ansible.

Running the azure_rm.py Python Script

Once we've installed the required software packages, we execute a test command that outputs a list of virtual machines deployed to Azure.

From within the ansible/ folder, which is where we have the script file. We execute a test command as shown in Listing 4-9.

Listing 4-9. Ansible Command Results That Lists All Virtual Machines Deployed to Azure

```
>$ ansible -i ansible/azure_rm.py spfarmstaging --list
  hosts (4):
    SP2012R2AD
    sp2016AppServer
    sp2016Sqlserver
    sp2016WFE
```

Another command available to us is

```
>$ ansible-inventory -i azure_rm.py –list
```

or if we wanted to show which hosts show up for specific groups, we can execute the following command, as well.

```
>$ ansible-inventory -i azure_rm.py –graph
```

We now see all the servers that we previously deployed using Terraform. Notice that the hostname corresponds to the name we provided for each virtual machine and not the actual computer name.

Use Ansible Playbooks to Install and Configure SharePoint 2016 Farm

Now that we have our infrastructure deployed via Terraform, it is time to start executing Ansible playbooks and tasks to perform configuration management. Specifically, we want to install the SharePoint 2016 and configure the farm topology.

Tip   We could have used built-in provisioners in Terraform to execute Ansible playbooks, but for our scenario, we want to keep Terraform usage to building out IaC and not perform any configuration management with it.

Execute Ansible Ad Hoc Commands Against Azure Virtual Machine

Before we get deep into executing Ansible playbooks against our Azure resources, we want to test basic commands to ensure that we have our setup properly configured.

Run Ansible's Setup Module via Ad Hoc Command

For this example, we will run the Ansible built-in setup module against the sp2016AppServeral already provisioned. This module gathers facts about the server in question. In our terminal, and while in the root of our GitHub project structure, we type what's shown in Listing 4-10.

Listing 4-10. Output of Executing an Ansible Setup Ad Hoc Command Against an Azure Virtual Machine

```
> $ ansible -i ansible/azure_rm.py sp2016AppServer -m setup -vvv --extra-
vars="ansible_user='packer' ansible_password='pass@word1!'"
ansible 2.4.3.0
  config file = /Users/sharepointoscar/git-repos/vagrant-ansible-packer-
  spfarm/ansible.cfg
  configured module search path = ['/Users/sharepointoscar/.ansible/
  plugins/modules', '/usr/share/ansible/plugins/modules']
  ansible python module location = /usr/local/lib/python3.6/site-packages/
  ansible
  executable location = /usr/local/bin/ansible
  python version = 3.6.4 (default, Jan  3 2018, 12:27:11) [GCC 4.2.1
  Compatible Apple LLVM 9.0.0 (clang-900.0.39.2)]
Using /Users/sharepointoscar/git-repos/vagrant-ansible-packer-spfarm/
ansible.cfg as config file
Parsed /Users/sharepointoscar/git-repos/vagrant-ansible-packer-spfarm/
ansible/azure_rm.py inventory source with script plugin
META: ran handlers
Using module file /usr/local/lib/python3.6/site-packages/ansible/modules/
windows/setup.ps1
<40.78.100.40> ESTABLISH WINRM CONNECTION FOR USER: packer on PORT 5985 TO
40.78.100.40
```

```
EXEC (via pipeline wrapper)
sp2016AppServer | SUCCESS => {
    "ansible_facts": {
        "ansible_architecture": "64-bit",
        "ansible_bios_date": "06/02/2017",
        "ansible_bios_version": "090007 ",
        "ansible_date_time": {
            "date": "2018-02-09",
            "day": "09",
            "epoch": "1518216073.77164",
            "hour": "22",
            "iso8601": "2018-02-09T22:41:13Z",
            "iso8601_basic": "20180209T224113771639",
            "iso8601_basic_short": "20180209T224113",
            "iso8601_micro": "2018-02-09T22:41:13.771639Z",
            "minute": "41",
            "month": "02",
            "second": "13",
            "time": "22:41:13",
            "tz": "UTC",
            "tz_offset": "+00:00",
            "weekday": "Friday",
            "weekday_number": "5",
            "weeknumber": "5",
            "year": "2018"
        },
        "ansible_distribution": "Microsoft Windows Server 2016 Datacenter",
        "ansible_distribution_major_version": "10",
        "ansible_distribution_version": "10.0.14393.0",
        "ansible_domain": "",
        "ansible_env": {
            "ALLUSERSPROFILE": "C:\\ProgramData",
            "APPDATA": "C:\\Users\\packer\\AppData\\Roaming",
            "COMPUTERNAME": "APPSERVER1",
            "ChocolateyInstall": "C:\\ProgramData\\chocolatey",
```

```
"ComSpec": "C:\\Windows\\system32\\cmd.exe",
"CommonProgramFiles": "C:\\Program Files\\Common Files",
"CommonProgramFiles(x86)": "C:\\Program Files (x86)\\Common
Files",
"CommonProgramW6432": "C:\\Program Files\\Common Files",
"HOMEDRIVE": "C:",
"HOMEPATH": "\\Users\\packer",
"LOCALAPPDATA": "C:\\Users\\packer\\AppData\\Local",
"LOGONSERVER": "\\\\APPSERVER1",
"NUMBER_OF_PROCESSORS": "2",
"OS": "Windows_NT",
"PATHEXT": ".COM;.EXE;.BAT;.CMD;.VBS;.VBE;.JS;.JSE;.WSF;.WSH;.
MSC;.CPL",
"PROCESSOR_ARCHITECTURE": "AMD64",
"PROCESSOR_IDENTIFIER": "Intel64 Family 6 Model 63 Stepping 2,
GenuineIntel",
"PROCESSOR_LEVEL": "6",
"PROCESSOR_REVISION": "3f02",
"PROMPT": "$P$G",
"PSExecutionPolicyPreference": "Unrestricted",
"PSModulePath": "C:\\Users\\packer\\Documents\\
WindowsPowerShell\\Modules;C:\\Program Files\\
WindowsPowerShell\\Modules;C:\\Windows\\system32\\
WindowsPowerShell\\v1.0\\Modules;C:\\Program Files\\Microsoft
Monitoring Agent\\Agent\\PowerShell",
"PUBLIC": "C:\\Users\\Public",
"Path": "C:\\Windows\\system32;C:\\Windows;C:\\Windows\\
System32\\Wbem;C:\\Windows\\System32\\WindowsPowerShell\\
v1.0\\;C:\\ProgramData\\chocolatey\\bin;C:\\Users\\packer\\
AppData\\Local\\Microsoft\\WindowsApps",
"ProgramData": "C:\\ProgramData",
"ProgramFiles": "C:\\Program Files",
"ProgramFiles(x86)": "C:\\Program Files (x86)",
"ProgramW6432": "C:\\Program Files",
"SystemDrive": "C:",
```

```
        "SystemRoot": "C:\\Windows",
        "TEMP": "C:\\Users\\packer\\AppData\\Local\\Temp",
        "TMP": "C:\\Users\\packer\\AppData\\Local\\Temp",
        "USERDOMAIN": "APPSERVER1",
        "USERDOMAIN_ROAMINGPROFILE": "APPSERVER1",
        "USERNAME": "packer",
        "USERPROFILE": "C:\\Users\\packer",
        "windir": "C:\\Windows"
    },
    "ansible_fqdn": "APPSERVER1.",
    "ansible_hostname": "APPSERVER1",
    "ansible_interfaces": [
        {
            "default_gateway": "10.10.1.1",
            "dns_domain": "3zqukdajuwtutf32mpr3kqjdlc.dx.internal.
            cloudapp.net",
            "interface_index": 3,
            "interface_name": "Microsoft Hyper-V Network Adapter #4",
            "macaddress": "00:0D:3A:36:EF:10"
        }
    ],
    "ansible_ip_addresses": [
        "10.10.1.5",
        "fe80::543e:c031:e4f0:773c"
    ],
    "ansible_kernel": "10.0.14393.0",
    "ansible_lastboot": "2018-02-09 21:11:13Z",
    "ansible_machine_id": "S-1-5-21-2571558981-2393378056-3617554007",
    "ansible_memtotal_mb": 7168,
    "ansible_nodename": "APPSERVER1.",
    "ansible_os_family": "Windows",
    "ansible_os_name": "Microsoft Windows Server 2016 Datacenter",
    "ansible_owner_contact": "",
    "ansible_owner_name": "",
    "ansible_powershell_version": 5,
    "ansible_processor": [
```

```
            "GenuineIntel",
            "Intel(R) Xeon(R) CPU E5-2673 v3 @ 2.40GHz",
            "GenuineIntel",
            "Intel(R) Xeon(R) CPU E5-2673 v3 @ 2.40GHz"
        ],
        "ansible_processor_cores": 2,
        "ansible_processor_count": 1,
        "ansible_processor_threads_per_core": 1,
        "ansible_processor_vcpus": 2,
        "ansible_product_name": "Virtual Machine",
        "ansible_product_serial": "0000-0007-6789-2939-5396-6604-04",
        "ansible_reboot_pending": false,
        "ansible_swaptotal_mb": 0,
        "ansible_system": "Win32NT",
        "ansible_system_description": "",
        "ansible_system_vendor": "Microsoft Corporation",
        "ansible_uptime_seconds": 5401,
        "ansible_user_dir": "C:\\Users\\packer",
        "ansible_user_gecos": "",
        "ansible_user_id": "packer",
        "ansible_user_sid": "S-1-5-21-2571558981-2393378056-3617554007-500",
        "ansible_win_rm_certificate_expires": "2018-02-10 02:12:35",
        "ansible_windows_domain": "WORKGROUP",
        "module_setup": true
    },
    "changed": false
}
META: ran handlers
META: ran handlers
```

Success! You might have noticed that the ad hoc command that we executed contains the Ansible -extra-vars populated with the domain username and password. We need to indicate this. Those credentials are different from the values found in the YAML file located at ansible/group_vars/all/all.yml. Specifically, the ansible_user and ansible_password values are different because they are used by the development environment.

> **Note**   You can change the ansible_user and ansible_password values found at an ansible/group_vars/all/all.yml to avoid adding those to ad hoc commands.

Resolving Errors

Inevitably, we are bound to get errors when we are first setting up our environment to execute commands against Azure, as there may be either outdated or missing libraries.

Error: *"winrm or requests is not installed: No module named xmltodict"*

```
$ ansible -i ansible/ec2.py -m ping tag_Role_AppServer --extra-
vars="ansible_port='5986' ansible_user='Administrator'ansible_
password='Pass@word1!'ansible_winrm_scheme='https' ansible_winrm_server_
cert_validation='ignore'" -vvvv
. . .
Using module file /Library/Python/2.7/site-packages/ansible/modules/system/
ping.py
52.53.237.25 | FAILED! => {
    "msg": "winrm or requests is not installed: No module named xmltodict"
}
```

Resolution

To resolve this error, run the following.

```
>$ pip install xmltodict
Collecting xmltodict
  Downloading xmltodict-0.11.0-py2.py3-none-any.whl
Installing collected packages: xmltodict
Successfully installed xmltodict-0.11.0
```

Error: *"winrm or requests is not installed: No module named winrm"*

One of the first errors we get from running our ping Ansible command, is shown in bold, as follows.

```
ansible 2.4.2.0
  . . .
```

```
Using module file /Library/Python/2.7/site-packages/ansible/modules/system/
ping.py
```
52.53.237.25 | FAILED! => {
      "msg": "winrm or requests is not installed: No module named winrm"
}

Resolution

This error is telling us that the pywinrm package is missing or not installed, essentially. This can happen if the Ansible Python executable is different from the one used on your terminal.

   If you have different Python interpreter versions (which happens often, and it is needed at times), then simply make sure that the pywinrm package is installed for that version. Run the following command.

```
>$ pip install pywinrm
Collecting pywinrm
  Downloading pywinrm-0.2.2-py2.py3-none-any.whl
Collecting requests-ntlm>=0.3.0 (from pywinrm)
  Downloading requests_ntlm-1.1.0-py2.py3-none-any.whl
Requirement already satisfied: xmltodict in /Library/Python/2.7/site-
packages (from pywinrm)
Collecting requests>=2.9.1 (from pywinrm)
  Downloading requests-2.18.4-py2.py3-none-any.whl (88kB)
    100%
|███████████████████████████████████████████████████████████████████|
92kB 3.0MB/s
Requirement already satisfied: six in /Library/Python/2.7/site-packages/
six-1.11.0-py2.7.egg (from pywinrm)
```

Errors: Ansible Command hangs for a long time

At times, executing an Ansible command may take a long time, and you get a timeout error message.

Resolution

First, test WinRM connectivity. From OS X, execute the following command.

```
>$ nc -z -w1 <HOSTNAME> 5985;echo $?
```

145

A successful output would look something like this.

```
>$ nc -z -w1 HOSTNAME 5985;echo $?
Connection to hostname port 5985 [tcp/wsman] succeeded!
0
```

If the command returns 0, then there are no WinRM connectivity issues, which tells us that there must be something wrong on the Ansible configuration side. Also ensure that WinRM is configured properly over the desired port: 5985 for HTTP and 5986 for HTTPS, which also requires certificates. In our scenario, it is critical that the Azure security group has the Ingress configured on the desired port.

If you still get connection refused errors, check the firewall rules on the host. In addition, since we are working with hosts in the cloud, you may need to adjust the scope of the Windows Remote Management (HTTP-in) rule to allow remote IPs to contact port 5985 on the public profile.

Run Ansible Playbooks by Role

Once we are past any connectivity issues on our virtual machines, we are ready to execute Ansible playbooks against our machines. We start with the domain controller, which is at the heart of our topology.

Warning   Before running any Ansible playbooks or commands, be sure to restart the Azure virtual machines. Somehow, we found that our Ansible playbook did not actually restart them when needed. To reboot via an Ansible command, you can execute the following command within the root of our project:>$ time Ansible all -I Ansible/azure_rm.py -e ansible_user=packer -e ansible_password=pass@word1! -m win_reboot.

Perform Configuration Management for the Domain Controller

We open a terminal and ensure that we are at the root of our GitHub repository.

```
>$ ansible-playbook -i ansible/azure_rm.py ansible/plays/domaincontroller.
yml --extra-vars="cloud_host='SP2012R2AD' ansible_user='packer' ansible_
password='pass@word1!'" -vvvv
```

As you can see, we are passing the administrator account and password as extra arguments. Of special interest, however, is the cloud_host variable. Our playbook accepts a parameter named cloud_host, which corresponds to the host we want to execute the playbook against.

After the playbook runs, the machine is promoted to a domain controller, and it is restarted.

The playbook will only execute the first task within our playbook. We must execute the second task, which adds the SharePoint service accounts and end-user sample accounts to AD once it is in place.

Note   The ansible_user and ansible_password variable values correspond to the Terraform defined in each virtual machine under os_profile.

A successful output will look similar to the following.

```
ansible-playbook 2.4.3.0
  config file = /Users/sharepointoscar/git-repos/vagrant-ansible-packer-
  spfarm/ansible.cfg
  configured module search path = ['/Users/sharepointoscar/.ansible/
  plugins/modules', '/usr/share/ansible/plugins/modules']
  ansible python module location = /usr/local/lib/python3.6/site-packages/
  ansible
  executable location = /usr/local/bin/ansible-playbook
  python version = 3.6.4 (default, Jan  3 2018, 12:27:11) [GCC 4.2.1
  Compatible Apple LLVM 9.0.0 (clang-900.0.39.2)]
Using /Users/sharepointoscar/git-repos/vagrant-ansible-packer-spfarm/
ansible.cfg as config file
setting up inventory plugins
Parsed /Users/sharepointoscar/git-repos/vagrant-ansible-packer-spfarm/
ansible/azure_rm.py inventory source with script plugin
..
statically imported: /Users/sharepointoscar/git-repos/vagrant-ansible-packer-
spfarm/ansible/roles/internal/domaincontroller/tasks/promote-domain.yml
statically imported: /Users/sharepointoscar/git-repos/vagrant-ansible-
packer-spfarm/ansible/roles/internal/domaincontroller/tasks/create-ad-
accounts.yml
```

```
Loading callback plugin default of type stdout, v2.0 from /usr/local/lib/
python3.6/site-packages/ansible/plugins/callback/default.py

PLAYBOOK: domaincontroller.yml
*************************************************************************
1 plays in ansible/plays/domaincontroller.yml
 [WARNING]: Could not match supplied host pattern, ignoring: |

 [WARNING]: Could not match supplied host pattern, ignoring:
DomainControllers

PLAY [domaincontroller.yml | All roles]
*************************************************************************
TASK [Gathering Facts]
*************************************************************************
Using module file /usr/local/lib/python3.6/site-packages/ansible/modules/
windows/setup.ps1
<104.210.33.93> ESTABLISH WINRM CONNECTION FOR USER: packer on PORT 5985 TO
104.210.33.93
checking if winrm_host 104.210.33.93 is an IPv6 address
EXEC (via pipeline wrapper)
ok: [SP2012R2AD]
META: ran handlers

TASK [domaincontroller : Install Active Directory on Windows Server 2016]
*************************************************************************
task path: /Users/sharepointoscar/git-repos/vagrant-ansible-packer-spfarm/
ansible/roles/internal/domaincontroller/tasks/promote-domain.yml:6
<104.210.33.93> ESTABLISH WINRM CONNECTION FOR USER: packer on PORT 5985 TO
104.210.33.93
checking if winrm_host 104.210.33.93 is an IPv6 address
EXEC (via pipeline wrapper)
EXEC (via pipeline wrapper)
<104.210.33.93> PUT "/Users/sharepointoscar/git-repos/vagrant-
ansible-packer-spfarm/ansible/roles/internal/domaincontroller/files/
create-domain.ps1" TO"C:\Users\packer\AppData\Local\Temp\ansible-
tmp-1518466688.0834079-241749603086064\create-domain.ps1"
```

```
EXEC (via pipeline wrapper)
EXEC (via pipeline wrapper)
ok: [SP2012R2AD] => {
    "changed": false,
    "rc": 0,
    "stderr": "The following exception occurred while retrieving
    member \"SetPassword\": \"The user name could not be found.\
    r\n\"\r\nAt C:\\Users\\packer\\AppData\\Local\\Temp\\ansible-
    tmp-1518466688.0834079-241749603086064\\create-domain.ps1:18
    char:3\r\n+     $adminUser.SetPassword($AutoLoginPassword)\r\
    n+     ~~~~~~~~~~~~~~~~~~~~~~~~~~~~~~~~~~~~~~~~~~\r\n+ CategoryInfo
    : NotSpecified: (:) [], ExtendedTypeSystemException\r\n+
    FullyQualifiedErrorId : CatchFromBaseGetMember\r\n",
    "stdout": "Configuring SharePoint Farm Active Directory Domain
    Controller\n  \r\nThe task has completed successfully.\r\nSee log
    %windir%\\security\\logs\\scesrv.log for detail info.\r\nCompleted
    5 percent (0/18) \tProcess Security Policy area
    \rCompleted 22 percent (3/18) \tProcess Security Policy area
    \rCompleted 44 percent (7/18) \tProcess Security Policy area
    \rCompleted 61 percent (10/18) \tProcess Security Policy area
    \rCompleted 77 percent (13/18) \tProcess Security Policy area
    \rCompleted 100 percent (18/18) \tProcess Security Policy area
    \r\r\nThe task has completed successfully.\r\nSee log %windir%\\
    security\\logs\\scesrv.log for detail info.\r\n\r\nSuccess Restart
    Needed Exit Code      Feature Result
    \r\n------- -------------- ---------      --------------
    \r\nTrue    No             Success       {Active Directory Domain
    Services, Group P...\r\n\r\nMessage      : You must restart this
    computer to complete the operation.\r\n      \r\nContext      :
    DCPromo.General.2\r\nRebootRequired : True\r\nStatus       :
    Success\r\n\r\n\r\n\r\n",
    "stdout_lines": [
        "Configuring SharePoint Farm Active Directory Domain Controller",
        "                                                                ",
        "The task has completed successfully.",
        "See log %windir%\\security\\logs\\scesrv.log for detail info.",
```

```
        "Completed 5 percent (0/18) \tProcess Security Policy area       ",
        "Completed 22 percent (3/18) \tProcess Security Policy area       ",
        "Completed 44 percent (7/18) \tProcess Security Policy area       ",
        "Completed 61 percent (10/18) \tProcess Security Policy area      ",
        "Completed 77 percent (13/18) \tProcess Security Policy area      ",
        "Completed 100 percent (18/18) \tProcess Security Policy area ",
        "                                                                 ",
        "The task has completed successfully.",
        "See log %windir%\\security\\logs\\scesrv.log for detail info.",
        "",
        "Success Restart Needed Exit Code      Feature Result             ",
        "------- --------------- ---------      --------------             ",
        "True    No              Success       {Active Directory
                                               Domain Services, Group P...",
        "",
        "Message        : You must restart this computer to
                          complete the operation.",
        "                 ",
        "Context        : DCPromo.General.2",
        "RebootRequired : True",
        "Status         : Success",
        "",
        "",
        ""

    ]

}
```

Next, we will execute the second portion of the playbook, which adds the required service accounts for SharePoint to Active Directory, as well as sample user accounts.

You may need to wait until the machine is fully restarted, or restart it manually using the Azure portal prior to executing the next playbook task. Be sure that you can RDP into it using the packer@sposcar.local domain account and the password, pass@word1!, prior to running Ansible tasks.

You may also execute the following Ansible command to test if the machine is up.

```
>$ ansible all -i ansible/azure_rm.py -e ansible_user=packer@sposcar.local
-e ansible_password=pass@word1! -m win_ping -l SP2012R2AD
```

Tip   Recall that we executed the same Ansible playbook in the Vagrant test environment that we built in Chapter 3. The difference now is that we are targeting the Azure virtual machine with the domain controller role. For information on the playbook content, go to `ansible/roles/domaincontroller/tasks/main.yml`.

```
> $ ansible-playbook -i ansible/azure_rm.py ansible/plays/domaincontroller.
yml --extra-vars="cloud_host='SP2012R2AD' ansible_user='packer@sposcar.
local' ansible_password='pass@word1!'" --start-at-task="Add Admin Account
to Domain Admins" -vvvvv
```

Because we promoted our Azure virtual machine to a domain controller in the previous execution of the Ansible playbook, we need to tell Ansible which credentials to use to perform configuration management, and use an account that has domain admin credentials. This account is the SPOSCAR\packer account, which is also the one we specified as an administrator when we baked the Packer image for our SharePoint farm.

Our playbook just added all the SharePoint service accounts in Active Directory and created sample users in Active Directory. After the Ansible task completes, our domain controller is ready for our SharePoint farm. Next, we configure the database server.

Perform Configuration Management for the Database Server

Because we are using an Azure-provided image for the SQL server role, we do not need to perform any configuration other than joining the VM to the domain. However, because we are using an Azure-provided SQL server image, we need to open the WinRM port to execute the Ansible playbook.

Note that we must enable the firewall port for the SQL server to be managed over WinRM, as the Azure gallery provided image has it closed by default. You have the option to automate this; in our case, we simply RDP to the VM and enable the firewall rule. It is port 5985 by default, and the rule is already created, so it is a matter of ensuring that it is enabled.

```
>$ ansible-playbook -i ansible/azure_rm.py ansible/plays/databaseservers.
yml --extra-vars="cloud_host='SP2016SQLSERVER' ansible_user='packer'
ansible_password='pass@word1!'" --tags="join-to-domain" -vvvv
```

To constrain our playbook from executing any other tasks, we use the Ansible "tags" and specify the value. Notice that we are using the non-domain VM administrative account to execute this task. The playbook task itself contains the proper domain account and password to allow for joining our VM to the domain. The playbook task can be found at `Ansible/Roles/Database/Task/main.yml`, where you can control which tasks are included in the playbook itself.

And that is it for our database server. It is now ready for our SharePoint install. But first, let's configure the other farm roles.

Perform Configuration Management for the App Server and WFE Roles

Our Ansible playbook is very much the same for both the app server and the WFE. The playbook contains two major tasks: one to join the machine to the domain and one to download and install the SharePoint prerequisites. It then runs AutoSPInstaller, which takes at least 40 minutes to finish executing.

```
> $ ansible-playbook -i ansible/azure_rm.py ansible/plays/appservers.yml
--extra-vars="cloud_host='sp2016AppServer' ansible_user='packer' ansible_
password='pass@word1!'" -vvvvv
```

Once the playbook completes, we should be able to access central administration on port 2016. If there are errors, we can see the script halting on our Ansible terminal. If there are errors, it is typically easier to RDP in to the VM and run the AutoSPInstaller to see the output from the script, as we don't get that within the Ansible terminal, unfortunately.

After the playbook runs, we execute a similar playbook for the WFE, as follows.

```
> $ ansible-playbook -i ansible/azure_rm.py ansible/plays/webservers.
yml --extra-vars="cloud_host='SP2016WFE' ansible_user='packer' ansible_
password='pass@word1!'" -vvvvv
```

Once the WFE playbook is completed, we have a clean SharePoint 2016 farm running, which can further be configured.

	NAME	TYPE ↑	LOCATION	KIND	ENVIRONMENT (...
	network-interface-spfarm-ad1	Network interface	West US		SharePoint 2(✎ 🗑 •••
	network-interface-spfarm-appserver1	Network interface	West US		SharePoint 2(✎ 🗑 •••
	network-interface-spfarm-db1	Network interface	West US		Staging ✎ 🗑 •••
	network-interface-spfarm-wfe1	Network interface	West US		Staging ✎ 🗑 •••
	spfarm-security-group-backend	Network security gr...	West US		Terraform De ✎ 🗑 •••
	spfarm-security-group-frontend	Network security gr...	West US		Terraform De ✎ 🗑 •••
	ad1-public-ip	Public IP address	West US		SharePoint 2(✎ 🗑 •••
	appserver1-public-ip	Public IP address	West US		SharePoint 2(✎ 🗑 •••
	db1-public-ip	Public IP address	West US		staging ✎ 🗑 •••
	wfe1-public-ip	Public IP address	West US		SharePoint 2(✎ 🗑 •••
	spfarmstaging	Storage account	West US	Storage	✎ •••
	SP2012R2AD	Virtual machine	West US		✎ •••
	sp2016AppServer	Virtual machine	West US		✎ •••
	SP2016SQLSERVER	Virtual machine	West US		✎ •••
	SP2016WFE	Virtual machine	West US		✎ •••
	spfarm_staging_network	Virtual network	West US		✎ •••

Figure 4-2. *Fully deployed SharePoint 2016 farm to the Azure cloud*

Summary

In this chapter, we walked through how to use IaC to provision a SharePoint 2016 farm to Azure in a consistent and repeatable way. We used Packer to create an Azure image that contains a couple of preinstalled packages, like VSCode in our example. We then referenced this custom VHD in our Terraform configuration files to provision our servers.

We also used Ansible to perform configuration management of our initial servers. Playbooks are a great way to have control over all configuration changes applied to the servers on our topology. Coupled with version control, it allows developers to make changes, test locally, execute targeting a staging environment, and then initiate pull requests prior to changes being pushed to a production environment.

In the next chapter, we create the proper artifacts in Packer and deploy our SharePoint 2016 farm to AWS.

## CHAPTER 5

Provisioning the SharePoint Farm to AWS Using Terraform and Ansible

In the previous chapter, we successfully created our golden image, the Windows machine that will be used to provision all the virtual machines in AWS and/or Azure.

In this chapter, we go through the exercise of deploying the SharePoint 2016 farm to a test environment in AWS using IaC. Once again, we use Terraform by HashiCorp.

About the Solution Architecture

Note that this architecture does not utilize some of the native AWS resources, such as AWS Directory Service or Amazon Relational Database Service (RDS). Although AWS Directory Service could be used with some modification to the domain controller Ansible configurations, RDS is not compatible because there are some permissions needed for SharePoint configuration that are not available.

© Oscar Medina, Ethan Schumann 2018
O. Medina and E. Schumann, *DevOps for SharePoint*, https://doi.org/10.1007/978-1-4842-3688-8_5

Caution   Note that we are creating the domain controller and database server in public subnets for ease of use, allowing us to run Ansible from our local machine without any additional VPN connections. In a production/live configuration, you want to configure a VPN to the VPC to run Ansible locally, or run Ansible on an instance that exists within the VPC. As shown in Figure 5-1, the private subnets are created but not used.

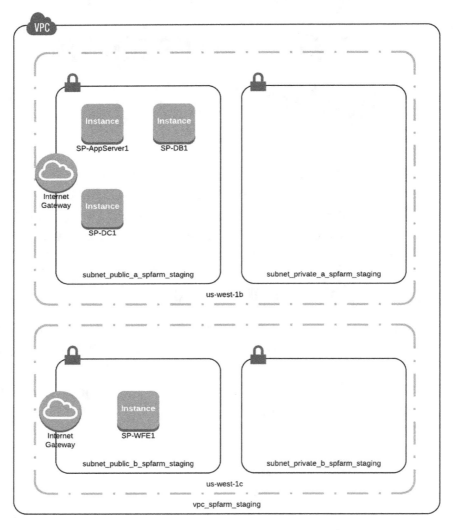

Figure 5-1.   *The AWS farm topology (similar to the Vagrant topology for dev environment)*

Terraform Folder Structure

Our Terraform folder is divided into environments. We have an AWS, a local, and a shared folder. The shared folder is where common artifacts are used by any environment. Items such as the SSH keys and providers reside within this folder.

```
> $ tree terraform -l 2
```

```
terraform
├── aws
│   ├── backend.tf
│   ├── environments
│   │   ├── staging
│   │   └── test
│   │       ├── backend.tf
│   │       ├── main.tf
│   │       └── variables.tf
│   ├── scripts
│   │   └── create-bucket.sh
├── azure
│   ├── environments
│   │   └── test
│   │       └── main.tf
│   └── terraform.tfstate.d
│       └── AZURE_SPFARM
├── local
│   └── variables.tf
├── shared
│   ├── providers
│   │   └── aws.tf
│   ├── ssh_keys
│   │   ├── keys.tf
│   │   ├── spfarm_rsa.pem
│   │   └── spfarm_rsa.pub
│   └── vpc
└── terraform.tfstate.d
```

```
2 [error opening dir]
```

```
16 directories, 21 filesTerraform project folder structure
```

For the purpose of going through the deployment of the SharePoint 2016 farm to AWS, we will mainly focus on the AWS folder contents within our GitHub repository throughout this exercise.

We will be building a fully functional SharePoint 2016 test environment in AWS.

Set up AWS Credentials

Terraform uses the AWS credentials already in our system. That is, we already have installed the AWS CLI and configured it using the `aws configure` command. Once AWS CLI is configured, the credentials are stored in the `~/.aws/credentials` file (on OS X). If you need to install AWS CLI on Windows or OS X, instructions are at `http://docs.aws. amazon.com/cli/latest/userguide/installing.html#install-msi-on-windows`.

Often, AWS engineers/operators have multiple accounts/access keys configured for executing against different accounts or with different permission levels. The core concepts of this practice are in the AWS documentation at `https://docs.aws.amazon. com/cli/latest/userguide/cli-multiple-profiles.html`.

The key takeaway for our work is knowing how to specify a profile when running your AWS CLI commands. This is as simple as using the `"--profile [PROFILE NAME]"` flag for all AWS commands; for example

```
aws s3api create-bucket --bucket $NAME --region $REGION --acl $ACL --
create-bucket-configuration LocationConstraint=$REGION --profile [PROFILE NAME].
```

Our exercises use a single profile in our AWS CLI config, so we have no need to use the `"--proflie"` flag.

Tip   Having AWS credentials configured prevents us from using them within our configuration, which should be avoided. Instead, Terraform reads the AWS credentials from our environment variables.

Configuring the Terraform Back End

Once we have the AWS CLI fully configured, we are ready to start working with Terraform. We must first set up storage and versioning of the Terraform state. Terraform state controls how changes to the infrastructure are tracked. In a team environment, this is a must-have for multiple team members making changes as part of the overall team workflow.

There are several of options when it comes to managing state for Terraform and setting up the back end. One option is to use the Terraform Enterprise product by HashiCorp. There are several others, including Consul, AzureRM, and Google Cloud.

The supported back end that we will use is the AWS S3 Bucket with versioning enabled, combined with DynamoDB to support state locking, as per the documentation.

Tip   To view a list of supported back ends, please visit `https://www.terraform.io/docs/backends/types/index.html`.

Create the S3 Bucket via AWS CLI

There are a couple of ways to create the S3 Bucket: via the web console or via the AWS CLI. Given that we already have the AWS CLI installed, we will use that approach. However, the outcome is the same, and you should use whichever approach you feel comfortable with.

We have created a Bash script to quickly create our bucket; it is located in the `terraform/aws/scripts` folder. Listing 5-1 shows what the Bash script looks like.

Caution   The Bash script is not meant to be robust, and can use enhancements to include error checking. However, it does successfully create the resources on AWS, as tested.

Listing 5-1. Utility Bash Script to Quickly Set up the Required S3 Bucket for the Terraform Back End

```
#!/bin/bash
set -e

while getopts n:r:a: option
do
```

```
 case "${option}"
 in
 n) NAME=${OPTARG};;
 r) REGION=${OPTARG};;
 a) ACL=$OPTARG;;
 esac
done

# We assume you have the AWS CLI installed.
aws s3api create-bucket --bucket $NAME --region $REGION --acl $ACL
--create-bucket-configuration LocationConstraint=$REGION

#enable versioning
aws s3api put-bucket-versioning --bucket $NAME --versioning-configuration
Status=Enabled

# Create AWS DynamoDB Table with Key for locking
aws dynamodb create-table --table-name terraform-lock --attribute-
definitions AttributeName=lockId,AttributeType=S --key-schema AttributeName
=lockId,KeyType=HASH --provisioned-throughput ReadCapacityUnits=1,WriteCapa
cityUnits=1
```

The script accepts three parameters, as follows:

- -n (this is the bucket name)

- -r (this is the region)

- -a (this is the ACL, acceptable values are private, public-read, public-read-write, and authenticated-read)

We give our bucket a meaningful name, spfarm-terraform-state, because we are considering using this bucket to storage of multiple environment Terraform states, such as dev, prod, and staging. We also set the region to us-west-1 region, which is US West Norcal. Lastly, we specify the ACL with a value of *private* for our purposes.

Tip   Setting the proper ACL on the Terraform state is critical, even within an organization. For more information, please refer to https://www.terraform.io/docs/state/sensitive-data.html.

Listing 5-2. Executing the Bash scripts outputs the results

```
> $ ./create-bucket.sh -n spfarm-terraform-state -r us-west-1 -a private
spfarm-terraform-staging
us-west-1
private{
    "Location": "http://spfarm-terraform-state.s3.amazonaws.com/"
}
{
    "TableDescription": {
        "TableArn": "arn:aws:dynamodb:us-west-1:653931956080:table/
        terraform-lock",
        "AttributeDefinitions": [
            {
                "AttributeName": "lockId",
                "AttributeType": "S"
            }
        ],
        "ProvisionedThroughput": {
            "NumberOfDecreasesToday": 0,
            "WriteCapacityUnits": 1,
            "ReadCapacityUnits": 1
        },
        "TableSizeBytes": 0,
        "TableName": "terraform-lock",
        "TableStatus": "CREATING",
        "KeySchema": [
            {
                "KeyType": "HASH",
                "AttributeName": "lockId"
            }
        ],
        "ItemCount": 0,
        "CreationDateTime": 1511986629.86
    }
}
```

The Bash script also enables versioning on our newly created S3 Bucket. In addition, it creates the DynamoDB Table with the proper configuration for locking the Terraform state.

Run Terraform Init

Now that we created our AWS S3 Bucket, we need to initialize Terraform for the AWS environment. Because we organized our Terraform folder by environment (AWS, Local, Azure, etc.), we want to ensure that we are within the `terraform/aws/environments/test` folder prior to running the command. In this scenario, we are building a staging environment on AWS for our SharePoint 2016 farm.

Note   Terraform also has the concept of workspaces, but we do not use them for our exercise. You can learn more about workspaces at `www.terraform.io/docs/state/workspaces.html`.

```
>$ terraform init
```

If successful, the output of this command should look like Listing 5-3.

Listing 5-3. Successful Console Output from Running the terraform init Command

```
me@sharepointoscar ~/git-repos/vagrant-ansible-packer-spfarm/terraform/aws/
environments/test
> $ terraform init

Initializing the backend...

Initializing provider plugins...
  - Checking for available provider plugins on https://releases.hashicorp.com...
  - Downloading plugin for provider "aws" (1.4.0)...

The following providers do not have any version constraints in
configuration, so the latest version was installed.

To prevent automatic upgrades to new major versions that may contain
breaking changes, it is recommended to add version = "..." constraints to
the corresponding provider blocks in configuration, with the constraint
strings suggested below.
```

```
* provider.aws: version = "~> 1.4"
```

Terraform has been successfully initialized!

You may now begin working with Terraform. Try running "terraform plan" to see any changes that are required for your infrastructure. All Terraform commands should now work.

If you ever set or change modules or backend configuration for Terraform, rerun this command to reinitialize your working directory. If you forget, other commands will detect it and remind you to do so if necessary.

The output is quite helpful, actually. There are two takeaways from this output that we can spot. The first thing is that Terraform is downloading the AWS provider. As of Terraform v0.10, the providers have been decoupled for good reasons. One reason is version constraint for a given solution. The following is a blurb from the announcement by HashiCorp:

> *As of v0.10, provider plugins are no longer included in the main Terraform distribution. Instead, they are distributed separately and installed automatically by the terraform init command.*

> *In the long run, this new approach should be beneficial to anyone who wishes to upgrade a specific provider to get new functionality without also upgrading another provider that may have introduced incompatible changes. In the short term, it just means a smaller distribution package and thus avoiding the need to download tens of providers that may never be used.*

Second, we can constraint the AWS provider to a specific version moving forward. For us, this means going into our provider file located at `terraform/shared/providers/aws.tf`, and adding the snippet of code suggested. Our file should look like Listing 5-4.

Listing 5-4. Contents of the aws.tf Provider File Constraining the Version of the AWS Provider for Our Solution

```
provider.aws: version = "~> 1.4"
provider "aws" {
  region     = "${var.aws_region}"
  access_key = "${var.aws_access_key_id}"
  secret_key = "${var.aws_secret_access_key}"
}
```

Define the Terraform Back End

Now that we have configured state and initialized Terraform, we are ready to define our back end declaratively using the HCL syntax. This file can be found under `terraform/aws/environments/test/backend.tf`. It should look similar to Listing 5-5.

Listing 5-5. The Terraform Back End Configuration File Contents (terraform/aws/environments/test/backend.tf)

```
terraform {
    backend "s3" {
        bucket          = "spfarm-terraform-state"
        key             = "shared/terraform_staging_env.tfstate"
        region          = "us-west-1"
        encrypt         = true
        dynamodb_table  = "terraform-lock"
    }
}
```

Perhaps you are wondering why we are not using interpolation when defining the back end. Unfortunately, Terraform back-end configuration does not support interpolation given the timing of the `init` command, by default. The initialization happens at such an early stage that interpolation is not yet available. If you would like to use interpolation with Terraform init, a partial initialization can be utilized to accomplish this by issuing the `"-backend-config"` command, in which you pass in the parameters via the CLI. The following is an example.

```
terraform init \
    -backend-config "bucket=$TF_VAR_tf_state_bucket" \
    -backend-config "lock_table=$TF_VAR_tf_state_table" \
    -backend-config "region=$TF_VAR_region" \
    -backend-config "key=$TF_VAR_application/$TF_VAR_environment"
```

Note that in this example, we are setting the values of the `init` flags using the same environment variables that we use to dynamically configure our Terraform variables. Environment variables can be easily injected into most environments. They allow us to create a common workflow, whether we are running locally or using continuous integration.

Excluding the use of "-backend-config", we must manually type the values and ensure that they match the S3 Bucket name and the DynamoDB Table name that we previously configured. This is the approach used throughout our examples.

Create Core AWS Resources Using Terraform

We have finally initialized our AWS environment and are ready to start defining our SharePoint 2016 farm Resources. Terraform uses HCL, or HashiCorp Configuration Language syntax. In HashiCorp's own words:

> *"HCL (HashiCorp Configuration Language) is a configuration language built by HashiCorp. The goal of HCL is to build a structured configuration language that is both human and machine friendly for use with command-line tools, but specifically targeted towards DevOps tools, servers, etc. HCL is also fully JSON compatible. That is, JSON can be used as completely valid input to a system expecting HCL. This helps makes systems interoperable with other systems."*

(https://github.com/hashicorp/hcl)

The first artifacts that we need to create (and this is typical) are the VPC, a security group, and any variables and output we would like to see at the time of running Terraform apply.

About Terraform Modules

Throughout this exercise, we use Terraform modules, which are hosted on a separate repository. Think of modules as reusable components that can be used throughout your AWS environments. Modules may contain attributes that are populated via static text or dynamically via setting the corresponding variable's value. Module sources supported include local, HashiCorp Registry, GitHub, HTTP URLs, and S3 Buckets.

For our exercise, we want to keep our modules versioned on GitHub. They are located at github.com/SharePointOscar/terraform_modules.git. We will reference them directly from there. So, let's get started.

Because we have our Terraform modules completely decoupled from our SharePoint 2016 Terraform project, we are able to modify the modules separately, and even version them or apply releases.

This can prove to be very powerful, as we might encounter a scenario where our SharePoint Terraform project depends on a specific release of, let's say, the AWS VPC module; in such case, we would want to specify the release within the module source. The following exercise walks you through the process of versioning the AWS VPC module within our GitHub repository.

VERSIONING THE AWS VPC MODULE

So, let's modify the AWS VPC module within our GitHub repository located at `https://github.com/SharePointOscar/terraform_modules.git`. Please clone it if you are following along. We will add the optional attribute, called enable_classiclink, for the sole purpose of demonstrating the versioning of modules. The code is shown in bold in the following.

```
resource "aws_vpc" "main" {
  cidr_block            = "${var.cidr_block}"
  instance_tenancy      = "${var.instance_tenancy}"
  enable_dns_support    = "${var.dns_support}"
  enable_dns_hostnames = "${var.dns_hostnames}"
  enable_classiclink    = "${var.enable_classiclink}"

  tags {
    Name = "${var.vpc_name}"
  }
}
```

Next, we add the corresponding variable in the vars.tf file, as shown in bold.

```
variable "vpc_name" {
  description = "VPC Name"
}
variable "enable_classiclink" {
  description = "Whether or not the VPC has Classiclink enabled"
}
variable "cidr_block" {
  description = "The CIDR block for the VPC"
}
```

```
variable "instance_tenancy" {
  description = "A tenancy option for instances launched into the VPC"
}

variable "dns_support" {
  description = "A tenancy option for instances launched into the VPC"
}

variable "dns_hostnames" {
  description = "A tenancy option for instances launched into the VPC"
}
```

Now that we have modified the VPC module, we want to version it; or in GitHub terms, create a release. To do this, we execute the following command.

```
>$ git tag -a "v0.0.1" -m "First release of the AWS VPC"

> $ git push --follow-tags
Counting objects: 1, done.
Writing objects: 100% (1/1), 180 bytes | 180.00 KiB/s, done.
Total 1 (delta 0), reused 0 (delta 0)
To https://github.com/SharePointOscar/terraform_modules.git
 * [new tag]           v0.0.1 -> v0.0.1
```

We now see that the tag has been created. This should also be visible within the GitHub UI. We can now reference the specific tag when creating the VPC, as shown in our next section.

Defining the Core Networking Resources

One of the first components we need to define is our virtual private cloud (VPC). There are interrelated components that we will also cover.

We define the core VPC, Internet gateway, firewall rules, and ports (as follows), which reside within the terraform/aws/environments/test/main.tf file.

Notice that we are pulling the specific VPC module version, and we have used the attribute (enable_classiclink) that we defined earlier.

```
module "vpc_spfarm_test" {
  source ="github.com/SharePointOscar/terraform_modules.git//aws_modules//
        vpc?ref=v0.0.1"
  vpc_name            = "vpc_spfarm_test"
```

```
  cidr_block         = "10.10.0.0/16"
  instance_tenancy = "default"
  dns_support        = true
  dns_hostnames      = true
  enable_classiclink = false
}

module "internet_gateway" {
  source    = "github.com/SharePointOscar/terraform_modules.git//aws_
              modules//internet_gateway"
  vpc_id    = "${module.vpc_spfarm_test.id}"
  igw_name = "gw_internet"
}

module "route_table" {
  source = "github.com/SharePointOscar/terraform_modules.git//aws_modules//
           route_table"
  vpc_id = "${module.vpc_spfarm_test.id}"
}

module "route" {
  source                  = "github.com/SharePointOscar/terraform_modules.
                            git//aws_modules//route"
  route_table_id          = "${module.route_table.route_table_id}"
  destination_cidr_block = "0.0.0.0/0"
  gateway_id              = "${module.internet_gateway.id}"
}
# Declare the data source
data "aws_availability_zones" "available" {}

module "subnet-public-a" {
  source            = "github.com/SharePointOscar/terraform_modules.git//
                      aws_modules//subnet"
  subnet_name       = "subnet_public_a_spfarm_test"
  availability_zone = "${data.aws_availability_zones.available.names[0]}"
  vpc_id            = "${module.vpc_spfarm_test.id}"
```

```
  cidr_block           = "10.10.1.0/24"
  map_public_ip_on_launch = "true"
}

module "subnet-public-b" {
  source               = "github.com/SharePointOscar/terraform_modules.git//
                           aws_modules//subnet"
  subnet_name          = "subnet_public_b_spfarm_test"
  availability_zone = "${data.aws_availability_zones.available.names[1]}"
  vpc_id               = "${module.vpc_spfarm_test.id}"
  cidr_block           = "10.10.2.0/24"
  map_public_ip_on_launch = "true"
}

module "subnet-private-a" {
  source               = "github.com/SharePointOscar/terraform_modules.git//
                           aws_modules//subnet"
  subnet_name          = "subnet_private_a_spfarm_test"
  availability_zone = "${data.aws_availability_zones.available.names[0]}"
  vpc_id               = "${module.vpc_spfarm_test.id}"
  cidr_block           = "10.10.4.0/24"
  map_public_ip_on_launch = "false"
}

module "subnet-private-b" {
  source               = "github.com/SharePointOscar/terraform_modules.git//
                           aws_modules//subnet"
  subnet_name          = "subnet_private_b_spfarm_test"
  availability_zone = "${data.aws_availability_zones.available.names[1]}"
  vpc_id               = "${module.vpc_spfarm_test.id}"
  cidr_block           = "10.10.5.0/24"
  map_public_ip_on_launch = "false"
}

module "route_table_association" {
  source           = "github.com/SharePointOscar/terraform_modules.git//aws_
                      modules//route_table_association"
```

```
  subnet_id      = "${module.subnet-public-a.id}"
  route_table_id = "${module.route_table.route_table_id}"
}

module "elb_security_group" {
  source  = "github.com/SharePointOscar/terraform_modules.git//aws_
            modules//security_group"
  sg_name = "sg_elb_spfarm_test"
  vpc_id  = "${module.vpc_spfarm_test.id}"
}

module "elb_http_rule" {
  source            = "github.com/SharePointOscar/terraform_modules.git//
                      aws_modules//security_group_rule"
  type              = "ingress"
  from_port         = 80
  to_port           = 80
  protocol          = "tcp"
  cidr_blocks       = ["0.0.0.0/0"]
  security_group_id = "${module.elb_security_group.id}"
}

module "sg_spfarm_test" {
  source  = "github.com/SharePointOscar/terraform_modules.git//
            aws_modules//security_group"
  sg_name = "sg_spfarm_test"
  vpc_id  = "${module.vpc_spfarm_test.id}"
}

# allow ssh connections
module "spfarm_test_ssh_rule" {
  source            = "github.com/SharePointOscar/terraform_modules.git//
                      aws_modules//security_group_rule"
  type              = "ingress"
  to_port           = 22
  from_port         = 22
  protocol          = "tcp"
  cidr_blocks       = ["0.0.0.0/0"]
```

```
  security_group_id = "${module.sg_spfarm_test.id}"
}

# allow ssh connections
module "spfarm_test_rdp_rule" {
  source            = "github.com/SharePointOscar/terraform_modules.git//
                       aws_modules//security_group_rule"
  type              = "ingress"
  to_port           = 3389
  from_port         = 3389
  protocol          = "tcp"
  cidr_blocks       = ["0.0.0.0/0"]
  security_group_id = "${module.sg_spfarm_test.id}"
}

# block all other ports
module "spfarm_test_egress_rule" {
  source            = "github.com/SharePointOscar/terraform_modules.git//
                       aws_modules//security_group_rule"
  type              = "egress"
  from_port         = 0
  to_port           = 0
  protocol          = "-1"
  cidr_blocks       = ["0.0.0.0/0"]
  security_group_id = "${module.sg_spfarm_test.id}"
}

module "elb_spfarm_test" {
  source              = "github.com/SharePointOscar/terraform_
                         modules.git//aws_modules//elb"
  elb_name            = "elb-spfarm-test"
  subnets             = ["${module.subnet-public-a.id}"]
  internal            = false
  security_groups     = ["${module.elb_security_group.id}"]
  instance_port       = 80
  instance_protocol   = "tcp"
  lb_port             = 80
```

```
    lb_protocol               = "tcp"
    healthy_threshold         = 2
    unhealthy_threshold       = 2
    timeout                   = 3
    target                    = "TCP:80"
    interval                  = 30
    cross_zone_load_balancing = true
}
```

Many foundational resources have been declared including security groups, security group rules, and public and private subnets. Had we not used Terraform modules, we would have repeated ourselves quite a bit in terms of declaring the same resources over and over again. Maintaining the code would prove to be an onerous task as our project grew.

To ensure that we get the modules registered within our solution, we must execute the terraform get command. Notice that it retrieves the specific tag for our VPC module.

```
> $ terraform get
- module.vpc_spfarm_test
  Getting source "github.com/SharePointOscar/terraform_modules.git//
  aws_modules//vpc?ref=v0.0.1"
- module.internet_gateway
- module.route_table
- module.route
- module.subnet-public-a
- module.subnet-public-b
- module.subnet-private-a
- module.subnet-private-b
- module.route_table_association
- module.elb_security_group
- module.elb_http_rule
- module.sg_spfarm_test
- module.spfarm_test_ssh_rule
- module.spfarm_test_rdp_rule
- module.spfarm_test_egress_rule
- module.elb_spfarm_test
- module.spfarmkeypair
- module.spfarm_WFE1
```

When we executed this command (and it has not been the first time), Terraform retrieved only the AWS VPC module since we explicitly asked for a version.

Tip   If you wish to refresh all modules, execute `terraform get -update=true`, which downloads all the modules.

Terraforming the SharePoint 2016 Servers in the Farm Topology

The next AWS resources that we need to define are the different virtual machines or instances. Recall that in Chapter 3, our topology included several server roles. We will define these same roles in Terraform to deploy them to AWS. We later use Ansible to perform configuration management, and install and configure SharePoint 2016, the domain controller, and the database server.

The following are the roles we will define via Terraform:

- Domain controller

- Database server

- Application server

- Web front end

Note   If you recall, in Chapter 3, we used Packer to create our "golden image," which is the AMI we use throughout our Terraform project to create AWS instances corresponding to the SharePoint server roles within the farm. However, we do *not* use our custom AMI for SQL, as we want to leverage the AMI from the gallery that contains the preinstalled SQL software.

Therefore, you will need to fetch the AMI ID that was produced with Packer, and add it to the variables.tf file. We will use it for the following parameter:

```
"DomainController" = "INSERT AMI HERE"

"AppServer"        = " INSERT AMI HERE "

"WFE"              = " INSERT AMI HERE "
```

All the instances use our custom AWS module, which allows us to really focus on the specific instance configuration, rather than figuring out how to define an instance. As an example of the configuration, we have the web front-end instance. Most of the attributes are populated from either variables within the `variables.tf` file, or a module's attribute value at runtime.

For example, you can see that `subnet_id` is populated from the *subnet* module. Likewise, the security group ID is populated from the security group module we declared and named `sg_spfarm_test` earlier within the file.

Of special interest is how the `availability_zone` attribute is populated using a *data module*, which we declared earlier in the `main.tf` file. We declared it as follows.

```
# Declare the data source
data "aws_availability_zones" "available" {}
```

The availability zones data module allows access to a list of AWS zones for the configured region at the provider level. In this case, our file located at `terraform/shared/providers/aws.tf`. This is quite helpful, since we may not remember what zone names are available, and we do not want to hard-code the values in our Terraform configuration. Listing 5-6 shows this module in action (code in bold). We simply get the first available value of the available zones.

Listing 5-6. Terraform AWS Instance Declaration for the SharePoint Web Front End

```
module "spfarm_WFE1" {
  source                      = "github.com/SharePointOscar/terraform_
                                 modules.git//aws_modules//instance"
  ami                         = "${lookup(var.ami, var.region)}"
  availability_zone           = "${data.aws_availability_zones.available.
                                 names[0]}"
  instance_type               = "${var.instance_type}"
  monitoring                  = true
  ebs_optimized               = falses
  associate_public_ip_address = true
  key_name                    = "${module.spfarmkeypair.key_name}"
  tenancy                     = "default"
  vpc_security_group_ids      = ["${module.sg_spfarm_test.id}"]
  subnet_id                   = "${module.subnet-public-a.id}"
```

```
instance_name              = "spfarm_WFE1"
volume_size                = "30"
volume_type                = "gp2"
iops                       = "100"
delete_on_termination      = true
}
```

Preparing to Deploy Resources to AWS

Now that we have all of our AWS SharePoint farm resources declared, it is time to deploy the resources. To do this, we first need to ensure that our configuration is validated by executing terraform validate.

Execute Terraform Plan

Terraform helps us plan the execution prior to changing infrastructure. When executed, the plan command generates an actual plan file that captures the exact changes that will be performed. It is a good practice to execute the plan command to ensure that all looks good. In addition, it is a great way to capture changes that may or may not need to be executed right away.

The terraform plan command accepts several optional parameters (you can type **terraform plan -h** to obtain a full list). Of special interest, is the –out=path because it allows you to specify the file in which you save the planned deployment. This file can then be used as input in executing the terraform apply command later.

```
>? terraform plan -out=aws_test_spfarm.plan
```

This outputs a long list of resources with values for some attributes, and others show <computed>, which is computed at runtime when you execute the terraform apply command. The following is a trimmed down look at our output, showing the WFE configuration.

```
Refreshing Terraform state in-memory prior to plan...
The refreshed state will be used to calculate this plan, but will not be
persisted to local or remote state storage.
```

```
data.aws_availability_zones.available: Refreshing state...

-----------------------------------------------------------------------

An execution plan has been generated and is shown below.
Resource actions are indicated with the following symbols:
  + create

Terraform will perform the following actions:

  . . .

  + module.spfarm_WFE1.aws_instance.main
      id:                                    <computed>
      ami:                                   "ami-955c6ef5"
      associate_public_ip_address:           "true"
      availability_zone:                     "us-west-1b"
      ebs_block_device.#:                    <computed>
      ebs_optimized:                         "false"
      ephemeral_block_device.#:              <computed>
      instance_state:                        <computed>
      instance_type:                         "t2.micro"
      ipv6_address_count:                    <computed>
      ipv6_addresses.#:                      <computed>
      key_name:                              "sp_farm_rsa"
      monitoring:                            "true"
      network_interface.#:                   <computed>
      network_interface_id:                  <computed>
      placement_group:                       <computed>
      primary_network_interface_id:          <computed>
      private_dns:                           <computed>
      private_ip:                            <computed>
      public_dns:                            <computed>
      public_ip:                             <computed>
      root_block_device.#:                   "1"
      root_block_device.0.delete_on_termination: "true"
```

```
    root_block_device.0.volume_size:        "30"
    root_block_device.0.volume_type:        "gp2"
    security_groups.#:                      <computed>
    source_dest_check:                      "true"
    subnet_id:                              "${var.subnet_id}"
    tags.%:                                 "1"
    tags.Name:                              "spfarm_WFE1"
    tenancy:                                "default"
    volume_tags.%:                          <computed>
    vpc_security_group_ids.#:               <computed>

  . . .

Plan: 20 to add, 0 to change, 0 to destroy.

------------------------------------------------------------------------

This plan was saved to: aws_test_spfarm.plan

To perform exactly these actions, run the following command to apply:
    terraform apply "aws_test_spfarm.plan"
```

Executing Terraform Apply

We've executed the terraform plan command and saved the proposed plan to a file. We like what we see and wish to now deploy all of the related resources to AWS. We do this by executing the following command.

```
>$ terraform apply aws_test_spfarm.plan
```

The output is quite lengthy, so we won't show you this. You should see all the resources created. Go to the AWS console to verify that all of our resources are created (see Figure 5-2).

Figure 5-2. *The four SharePoint EC2 instances we deployed using Terraform*

Caution   You may incur charges deploying resources to AWS. It is recommended that you destroy the resources as soon as possible to avoid charges.

We've gone through the process of deploying our entire SharePoint infrastructure to AWS, but we are not done yet! We need to now perform configuration management tasks using Ansible and with the same playbooks that we executed when building the Vagrant test environment for SharePoint in Chapter 3. Before that, we must ensure that Ansible has an inventory of the EC2 instances, including the IP addresses. In our next section, we cover how to generate an Ansible dynamic inventory from AWS resources.

Generating the Dynamic Ansible Inventory File for AWS Resources

Because we are using AWS EC2 instances, we expect that at any given point, we can tear down and re-create the instances, which means IP addresses will change. Therefore, instead of having a static Ansible inventory file, as we had for our Vagrant SharePoint test environment, we want to build it based on the existing EC2 instances in AWS.

Using EC2.py and EC2.ini Files Provided by Ansible

We could figure out how to build a dynamic inventory file for Ansible from scratch. But there is no need to do so, given that Ansible provides a Python script for us to use (`http://docs.ansible.com/ansible/latest/intro_dynamic_inventory.html#example-aws-ec2-external-inventory-script`).

First, download the two files into the project's Ansible folder and ensure that the `EC2.py` file is executable by using `chmod u+x ec2.py`.

`ec2.in` serves as a configuration file that can be customized; for example, we may not be using some of the services listed, so they can be commented out. As another example, we do not want RDS or ElastiCache, so we excluded them as shown in Listing 5-7.

Listing 5-7. Excluding Services Within the ec2.ini File

```
[ec2]
...

# To exclude RDS instances from the inventory, uncomment and set to False.
rds = False

# To exclude ElastiCache instances from the inventory, uncomment and set to
False.
elasticache = False
...
```

Note that, the ec2.py script has a dependency on Boto that requires the AWS credentials as it interacts with the AWS API; however, we are able to execute the ec2.py script against AWS without entering credentials because we have the `AWS_ACCESS_KEY_ID` and `AWS_SECRET_ACCESS_KEY` set in our environment already.

Installing Boto

In order to use the provided Python script, we need to ensure that Boto (an AWS SDK for Python) is installed. On OS X, it can be installed as follows.

```
>$ pip install boto
```

Note   If you have Boto3 installed, this script actually imports it for you automatically.

Running the EC2 Script

Once we've installed the required software packages, we execute a test command that outputs a list of instances with many of the metadata attributes.

From within the `ansible/` folder, which is where we have the script file, we execute the test command as shown in Listing 5-8.

Listing 5-8. Trimmed Output of the ./ec2.py –list Command. We Only Show an Instance and Its Metadata

```
>$ ec2.py --list
{
  "_meta": {
    "hostvars": {
      "54.219.142.97": {
        "ansible_host": "54.219.142.97",
. . .
        "ec2_tag_Environment": "Staging",
        "ec2_tag_Group": "DomainControllers",
        "ec2_tag_Name": "spfarm-SP-DC",
        "ec2_tag_Role": "DomainController",
        "ec2_virtualization_type": "hvm",
        "ec2_vpc_id": "vpc-fd1cfb9a"
    }
  }
},
```

```
  "ami_dc92a8bc": [
    "54.219.142.97"
  ],
"tag_Environment_Staging": [
    "54.219.142.97"
  ],
  "tag_Group_DomainControllers": [
    "54.219.142.97"
  ],
  "tag_Name_spfarm_SP_DC": [
    "54.219.142.97"
  ],
  "tag_Role_DomainController": [
    "54.219.142.97"
  ],
. . .
}
```

Note   Running the ec2.py script from outside EC2 is not efficient; typically, you want to run it within EC2, which also entails using the internal IP and DNS vs. public.

Use Ansible Playbooks to Install and Configure SharePoint 2016 Farm

Now that we have our infrastructure deployed via Terraform, it is time to start executing Ansible playbooks and tasks to perform configuration management. Specifically, we want to install SharePoint 2016 and configure the farm topology.

Tip   We could have used built-in provisioners in Terraform to execute Ansible playbooks, but for our scenario, we want to keep Terraform usage to building out IaC, not to perform any configuration management with it.

Execute Ansible Ad Hoc Commands Against AWS Instance

Before we get deep into executing Ansible playbooks against our AWS resources, we want
to test basic commands to ensure that we have our setup properly configured.

Obtaining EC2 Instances IP Addresses

Earlier, when we executed the `./ec2.py –list` command, we received a response
in JSON with details of all the AWS instances currently running. This information is
valuable, as we can obtain specific details to execute Ansible commands against a
specific server group, role, or machine. The output of the command looked something
like the following (trimmed for brevity).

```
. . .
{
  "_meta": {
    "hostvars": {
      "54.219.142.97": {
        "ansible_host": "54.219.142.97",
        "ec2__in_monitoring_element": false,
        "ec2_account_id": "653931956080",
        "ec2_ami_launch_index": "0",
        "ec2_architecture": "x86_64",
        "ec2_block_devices": {
          "sda1": "vol-0a344355d70b96b64"
        },
        "ec2_client_token": "",
        "ec2_dns_name": "ec2-54-219-142-97.us-west-1.compute.amazonaws.com",
        "ec2_ebs_optimized": false,
        "ec2_eventsSet": "",
        "ec2_group_name": "",
        "ec2_hypervisor": "xen",
        "ec2_id": "i-0f606be765e7f5bf2",
        "ec2_image_id": "ami-dc92a8bc",
        "ec2_instance_profile": "",
        "ec2_instance_type": "t2.micro",
        "ec2_ip_address": "54.219.142.97",
```

"ec2_item": "",
"ec2_kernel": "",
"ec2_key_name": "spfarm_rsa",
"ec2_launch_time": "2017-12-07T22:23:25.000Z",
"ec2_monitored": false,
"ec2_monitoring": "",
"ec2_monitoring_state": "disabled",
"ec2_persistent": false,
"ec2_placement": "us-west-1b",
"ec2_platform": "windows",
"ec2_previous_state": "",
"ec2_previous_state_code": 0,
"ec2_private_dns_name": "ip-10-10-1-50.us-west-1.compute.internal",
"ec2_private_ip_address": "10.10.1.50",
"ec2_public_dns_name": "ec2-54-219-142-97.us-west-1.compute.
amazonaws.com",
"ec2_ramdisk": "",
"ec2_reason": "",
"ec2_region": "us-west-1",
"ec2_requester_id": "",
"ec2_root_device_name": "/dev/sda1",
"ec2_root_device_type": "ebs",
"ec2_security_group_ids": "sg-90afb8f6",
"ec2_security_group_names": "sg_spfarm_staging",
"ec2_sourceDestCheck": "true",
"ec2_spot_instance_request_id": "",
"ec2_state": "running",
"ec2_state_code": 16,
"ec2_state_reason": "",
"ec2_subnet_id": "subnet-3ae93f61",
"ec2_tag_Environment": "Staging",
"ec2_tag_Group": "DomainControllers",
"ec2_tag_Name": "spfarm-SP-DC",
"ec2_tag_Role": "DomainController",
"ec2_virtualization_type": "hvm",

```
        "ec2_vpc_id": "vpc-fd1cfb9a"
      }
    }
  },
  "ami_dc92a8bc": [
    "54.219.142.97"
  ],
  "ec2": [
    "54.219.142.97"
  ],
  "i-0f606be765e7f5bf2": [
    "54.219.142.97"
  ],
  "key_spfarm_rsa": [
    "54.219.142.97"
  ],
  "platform_windows": [
    "54.219.142.97"
  ],
  "security_group_sg_spfarm_staging": [
    "54.219.142.97"
  ],
  "tag_Environment_Staging": [
    "54.219.142.97"
  ],
  "tag_Group_DomainControllers": [
    "54.219.142.97"
  ],
  "tag_Name_spfarm_SP_DC": [
    "54.219.142.97"
  ],
  "tag_Role_DomainController": [
    "54.219.142.97"
  ],
  "type_t2_micro": [
    "54.219.142.97"
```

```
  ],
  "us-west-1": [
    "54.219.142.97"
  ],
  "us-west-1b": [
    "54.219.142.97"
  ],
  "vpc_id_vpc_fd1cfb9a": [
    "54.219.142.97"
  ]
}
. . .
```

If you want to execute an Ansible playbook against all domain controllers, you can use the `tag_Group_DomainControllers` tag. If we had deployed multiple domain servers, we would have several IP addresses, and our Ansible command would target all servers in the group. Powerful, indeed.

Tip   When using the ec2 inventory script, hosts automatically appear in groups based on how they are tagged in EC2. This is why our Terraform declarations include specific tags such as *role* and *group* as well as *environment*—all for the purpose of filtering assets when executing Ansible tasks and playbooks against AWS instances.

Run Ansible's Setup Module via Ad Hoc Command

For this example, we use the `tag_Role_DomainController`, which we obtained from the output of our previous command, and run the Ansible built-in `setup` module against the server. This module gathers facts about the server in question. In our terminal, we type what's shown in Listing 5-9.

Listing 5-9. Output of Executing a Ping Against EC2 Instance

```
> $ ansible -i ansible/ec2.py -m setup tag_Role_DomainController –extra-
vars="ansible_user='vagrant@sposcar.local' ansible_password='Pass@word1!'"
-vvvvv

ansible 2.4.1.0
  config file = /Users/sharepointoscar/git-repos/vagrant-ansible-packer-
            spfarm/ansible.cfg
  configured module search path = [u'/Users/sharepointoscar/.ansible/
                              plugins/modules', u'/usr/share/ansible/
                              plugins/modules']
  ansible python module location = /usr/local/Cellar/ansible/2.4.1.0/
                              libexec/lib/python2.7/site-packages/
                              ansible
  executable location = /usr/local/bin/ansible
  python version = 2.7.14 (default, Sep 25 2017, 09:53:22) [GCC 4.2.1
                Compatible Apple LLVM 9.0.0 (clang-900.0.37)]
Using /Users/sharepointoscar/git-repos/vagrant-ansible-packer-spfarm/
ansible.cfg as config file
Reading vault password file: /Users/sharepointoscar/git-repos/vagrant-
ansible-packer-spfarm/vpass.txt
setting up inventory plugins
Parsed /Users/sharepointoscar/git-repos/vagrant-ansible-packer-spfarm/
ansible/ec2.py inventory source with script plugin
Loading callback plugin minimal of type stdout, v2.0 from /usr/local/
Cellar/ansible/2.4.1.0/libexec/lib/python2.7/site-packages/ansible/plugins/
callback/__init__.pyc
META: ran handlers
Using module file /usr/local/Cellar/ansible/2.4.1.0/libexec/lib/python2.7/
site-packages/ansible/modules/windows/setup.ps1
<54.219.142.97> ESTABLISH WINRM CONNECTION FOR USER: vagrant@sposcar.local
on PORT 5985 TO 54.219.142.97
<54.219.142.97> WINRM CONNECT: transport=ntlm endpoint=http://54.219.142.
                97:5985/wsman
<54.219.142.97> WINRM OPEN SHELL: 900867AA-E791-4474-ADDB-BE9F63583127
EXEC (via pipeline wrapper)
```

```
<54.219.142.97> WINRM EXEC 'PowerShell' ['-NoProfile', '-NonInteractive',
'-ExecutionPolicy', 'Unrestricted', '-']
<54.219.142.97> WINRM RESULT u'<Response code 1, out
"{"changed":false,"an", err "An error occurred wh">'
<54.219.142.97> WINRM CLOSE SHELL: 900867AA-E791-4474-ADDB-BE9F63583127
54.219.142.97 | SUCCESS => {
    "ansible_facts": {
        "ansible_architecture": "64-bit",
        "ansible_bios_date": "08/24/2006",
        "ansible_bios_version": "4.2.amazon",
. . .
"ansible_fqdn": "SP-DC.sposcar.local",
        "ansible_hostname": "SP-DC",
        "ansible_interfaces": [
            {
                "default_gateway": "10.10.1.1",
                "dns_domain": null,
                "interface_index": 4,
                "interface_name": "AWS PV Network Device #0",
                "macaddress": "06:28:3F:57:C6:72"
            }
        ],
        "ansible_ip_addresses": [
            "10.10.1.50",
            "fe80::c986:a7cb:c3dc:deb8"
        ],
. . .
},
    "changed": false,
    "failed": false
}
META: ran handlers
META: ran handlers
```

Success! You might have noticed that the ad hoc command we executed contains the Ansible –extra-vars populated with the domain username and password. We need to add this because the machine we are targeting is a domain controller.

Run Ansible Playbooks by Role

Now that we have tested our setup locally, we are ready to execute Ansible Playbooks by SharePoint specific role.

Perform Configuration Management for the Domain Controller

> **Tip**   If this is your first time running Ansible, you may need to install some prerequisite plug-ins. Most common are xmltodict and pywinrm, which can be installed via pip on any OS.
>
> ```
> pip install xmltodict
> pip install pywinrm
> ```

First, let's set up the domain controller. Notice that we are using the local administrator account for this run because the domain controller is not yet set up. For subsequent runs, we will use the credentials stored in the Ansible configuration.

There are two things to note if you are using macOS High Sierra. You may have to disable History Expansion in your bash terminal to get the exclamation point shown in the following password to work. This can be done with the "set +H" command.

Also, there is a known bug in which Python fails when trying to create a fork. This can be worked around with the "export OBJC_DISABLE_INITIALIZE_FORK_SAFETY=YES" command.

```
ansible-playbook -i ansible/ec2.py ansible/plays/domaincontroller.
yml --extra-vars="ec2_host='tag_Role_DomainController' ansible_user='.\
Administrator' ansible_password='Pass@word1!'" --tags="create-domain" -vvvv
```

After this first run, the machine is promoted to a domain controller, and it is restarted. Next, we execute the second portion of the playbook, which adds the required service accounts for SharePoint, as well as sample user accounts. Please note that the server may take some time (up to five minutes) to become ready for the following playbook. If you run the following commands before it is ready, you will receive an error.

Tip   Recall that we executed the same Ansible playbook in the Vagrant test environment we built in Chapter 3. The difference now is that we are targeting the EC2 instance with the DomainController role. For information on the playbook content, go to ansible/roles/domaincontroller/tasks/main.yml.

```
ansible-playbook -i ansible/ec2.py ansible/plays/domaincontroller.yml
--extra-vars="ec2_host='tag_Role_DomainController'" --start-at-task="Add
Admin Account to Domain Admins" -vvvvv
```

After this Ansible task has completed, our domain controller is ready for our SharePoint farm. Next, we configure the database server.

Perform Configuration Management for the Database Server

We will now join the database server to the domain using the following command. Since we are using an AWS-provided image that comes with SQL Server preinstalled, there is no need to configure the database.

```
ansible-playbook -i ansible/ec2.py ansible/plays/databaseservers.yml
--extra-vars="ec2_host='tag_Role_Database'" --tags="join-to-domain" -vvvvv
```

Perform Configuration Management for SharePoint Server

We now need to configure the SharePoint application server by joining it to the domain, downloading the SharePoint .img file from Microsoft, and running the AutoSPInstaller tool.

AutoSPInstaller is an open source project created by Brian Lalancette. It abstracts the installation of SharePoint to an XML configuration file and allows a completely unattended setup. Prior to the creation of the tool, this process was a huge boon to IT professionals who were trying to reliably deploy SharePoint in an automated fashion.

Our first step, like the other servers, is to join the domain.

```
ansible-playbook -i ansible/ec2.py ansible/plays/appservers.yml --extra-
vars="ec2_host='tag_Role_AppServer'" --tags="join-to-domain" -vvvvv
```

Once this is complete, we can execute the script to install SharePoint and get it up and running. This script leverages the open source project AutoSPInstaller, which is a fully unattended installation of SharePoint. Note that this script downloads the SharePoint installation media directly from Microsoft, which can take quite a while.

If we take a look at the Ansible scripts, we can see a few steps being conducted: installing PSExec, downloading SharePoint media from Microsoft, moving needed components to the C:\SP location, and installing all prerequisite Windows features. Once all of this is completed, we simply instruct Ansible to start the `AutoSPInstallerLaunch.bat` file, which runs the entire SharePoint installation process for us. Note that the installation does require a restart, so to ensure that Ansible is monitoring the process and reports upon completion, we use a `win_wait_for` step that periodically checks for the SharePoint administration port (2016) to come up and start listening for traffic. Once this is detected, Ansible will report a successful installation and exit gracefully.

```
ansible-playbook -i ansible/ec2.py ansible/plays/appservers.yml --extra-vars="ec2_host='tag_Role_AppServer' ansible_user='vagrant@sposcar.local' ansible_password='Pass@word1!'"  --start-at-task="Install PSExec" -vvvvv
```

Let's take a look at the Ansible script we are using to install SP. The following are the actions taken:

- Install PSExec.

- Download SharePoint from Microsoft to the host at C:\.

- Mount the SharePoint image to D:\ so the files can be accessed.

- Create the C:\SP directory and copy the necessary files from the image to this folder.

- Install all the prerequisites for the Microsoft packages needed for SharePoint.

- Launch the unattended SPAutoInstaller.

- Wait for SharePoint administration port 2016 to become available.

```
- name: Install PSExec
  win_chocolatey:
    name: psexec
  ignore_errors: yes

- name: Download SharePoint 2016
  win_get_url:
    url: https://download.microsoft.com/download/0/0/4/004EE264-7043-45BF-99E3-3F74ECAE13E5/officeserver.img
```

```
        dest: c:\
        force: no
# - name: Copy Officeserver.img to server
#   win_copy:
#      src: ../../common/files/officeserver.img
#      dest: c:\officeserver.img
#      force: no

# This task mounts the Officeserver.img file
- name: Mount the SharePoint Bits IMG
  win_disk_image:
      image_path: c:\officeserver.img
      state: present
  register: disk_image_out

- name: Create c:\SP directory
  win_file:
    path: C:\SP
    state: directory

- name: Copy SP folder (SPAutoInstaller folder structure)
  win_copy:
    src: ../../common/files/SP/
    dest: C:\SP
    force: false

- name: Copy SP Bits in D:\ to SPAutoInstaller folder structure
  win_shell: XCOPY D:\* C:\SP\2016\SharePoint\ /s /i /Y
  args:
  executable: cmd

- name: Unmount SharePoint Bits .img
  win_disk_image:
    image_path: c:\officeserver.img
    state: absent

- name: Install All Required Windows Features
  win_feature:
```

```
      name: NET-HTTP-Activation,NET-Non-HTTP-Activ,NET-WCF-Pipe-
      Activation45,NET-WCF-HTTP-Activation45,Web-Server,Web-WebServer,
      Web-Common-Http,Web-Static-Content,Web-Default-Doc,Web-Dir-Browsing,
      Web-Http-Errors,Web-App-Dev,Web-Asp-Net,Web-Asp-Net45,Web-Net-Ext,
      Web-Net-Ext45,Web-ISAPI-Ext,Web-ISAPI-Filter,Web-Health,Web-Http-
      Logging,Web-Log-Libraries,Web-Request-Monitor,Web-Http-Tracing,Web-
      Security,Web-Basic-Auth,Web-Windows-Auth,Web-Filtering,Web-Digest-Auth,
      Web-Performance,Web-Stat-Compression,Web-Dyn-Compression,Web-Mgmt-
      Tools,Web-Mgmt-Console,Web-Mgmt-Compat,Web-Metabase,WAS,WAS-Process-
      Model,WAS-NET-Environment,WAS-Config-APIs,Web-Lgcy-Scripting,Windows-
      Identity-Foundation,Xps-Viewer
      state: present
      restart: yes
      include_sub_features: yes
      include_management_tools: yes

# make sure to put the prerequisites in the proper folder.
- name: Download SharePoint Prerequisites
  script: ../../common/files/DownloadPrerequisites.ps1 -SPPrerequisitesPath
  {{SharePointPrerequisitesPath}}

- name: Install SharePoint Prerequisites via PowerShell
  script: ../../common/files/Install-Prerequisites.ps1 -SharePointBitsPath
  {{SharePointBitsPath}}

- name: Trigger AutoSPInstaller (computer will restart and continue install)
  win_shell: C:\SP\AutoSPInstaller\AutoSPInstallerMain.ps1 C:\SP\
  AutoSPInstaller\AutoSPInstallerInput.xml

# - name: Reboot after installing SPAutoInstaller pre-reqs
#   win_reboot:

- name: wait until admin port 2016 is available. start checking after 10
  minutes.
  win_wait_for:
    port: 2016
    state: present
```

```
delay: 600
sleep: 20
```

Once this script is complete, Ansible exits and shows that the preceding steps have succeeded. Note that SharePoint can take quite a bit of time to install, upwards of 20 to 30 minutes.

Perform Configuration Management for SharePoint Web Server

Our final step in this chapter is to configure the web servers for hosting the SharePoint application. As with the other servers, our first step is to join the domain we previously created.

```
ansible-playbook -i ansible/ec2.py ansible/plays/appservers.yml --extra-vars="ec2_host='tag_Role_WFE'" --tags="join-to-domain" -vvvvv
```

We now utilize a playbook identical to that of the main SharePoint server. Once again utilizing the AutoSPInstaller tool, we simply execute the Ansible playbook and let the scripts take care of the rest. A great feature of the AutoSPInstaller tool is that it automatically detects when another SharePoint server has been deployed, and then configures this instance to join the farm as a SharePoint web server.

```
ansible-playbook -i ansible/ec2.py ansible/plays/appservers.yml --extra-vars="ec2_host='tag_Role_WFE" --start-at-task="Install PSExec" -vvvvv
```

Validating the Installation

With this final task complete, we can now navigate to the public IP address of either of the SharePoint servers at port 2016 to see that the site is running in the default configuration state (see Figure 5-3).

Figure 5-3. *The SharePoint Farm is up and running, Central Administration Console accessed via the browser*

Resolving Errors

Inevitably, we are bound to get errors when we are first setting up our environment to execute commands against AWS, as there may be either outdated or missing libraries.

Error: "winrm or requests is not installed: No module named xmltodict"

```
$ ansible -i ansible/ec2.py -m ping tag_Role_AppServer --extra-
vars="ansible_port='5986' ansible_user='Administrator'ansible_
password='Pass@word1!'ansible_winrm_scheme='https' ansible_winrm_server_
cert_validation='ignore'" -vvvv
. . .
Using module file /Library/Python/2.7/site-packages/ansible/modules/system/
ping.py
52.53.237.25 | FAILED! => {
    "msg": "winrm or requests is not installed: No module named xmltodict"
}
```

Resolution

To resolve this error, run the following.

```
>$ pip install xmltodict
Collecting xmltodict
  Downloading xmltodict-0.11.0-py2.py3-none-any.whl
Installing collected packages: xmltodict
Successfully installed xmltodict-0.11.0
```

Error: "winrm or requests is not installed: No module named winrm"

One of the first errors we get from running our ping Ansible command is shown in bold in the following.

```
ansible 2.4.2.0
  . . .
Using module file /Library/Python/2.7/site-packages/ansible/modules/system/
ping.py
52.53.237.25 | FAILED! => {
    "msg": "winrm or requests is not installed: No module named winrm"
}
```

Resolution

This error is telling us that the pywinrm package is missing or not installed essentially. This can happen if the Ansible Python executable is different from the one used on your terminal.

If you have different Python interpreter versions (which happens often, and it is needed at times), then simply make sure that the pywinrm package is installed for the version. Run the following command.

```
>$ pip install pywinrm
Collecting pywinrm
  Downloading pywinrm-0.2.2-py2.py3-none-any.whl
Collecting requests-ntlm>=0.3.0 (from pywinrm)
  Downloading requests_ntlm-1.1.0-py2.py3-none-any.whl
Requirement already satisfied: xmltodict in /Library/Python/2.7/site-
packages (from pywinrm)
```

```
Collecting requests>=2.9.1 (from pywinrm)
  Downloading requests-2.18.4-py2.py3-none-any.whl (88kB)
    100% |████████████████████████████████| 92kB 3.0MB/s
Requirement already satisfied: six in /Library/Python/2.7/site-packages/
six-1.11.0-py2.7.egg (from pywinrm)
```

Errors: Ansible Command hangs for a long time

At times, executing an Ansible command may take a long time, and you get a timeout error message.

Resolution

First, test WinRM connectivity. From OS X, execute the following command.

```
>$ nc -z -w1 <HOSTNAME> 5985;echo $?
```

If the command returns 0, then there are no WinRM connectivity issues, which tells us that there must be something wrong on the Ansible configuration side. Also, ensure that WinRM is configured properly over the desired ports: 5985 for HTTP and 5986 for HTTPS, which also requires certificates. In our scenario, it is critical to ensure that the AWS security group has the Ingress configured on the desired port.

Tip   Please ensure that the WinRM listener is actually listening on the correct port. Also note, we use port 5985, though in production you may want to use port 5986 which encrypts traffic. Lastly, ensure that Windows Firewall is allowing access via the domain public profile (this tends to be missed).

Summary

In this chapter, we walked through how to deploy and configure a SharePoint farm in AWS using Terraform for infrastructure provisioning, and Ansible for configuration management. With Terraform, we deployed all the resources required for a functioning farm: an AWS VPC including subnets, internet gateways, security groups, one SQL Server database, one SharePoint application server, and one SharePoint web server. This setup provides us with a functional base installation of SharePoint.

In the next chapter, we explore the configuration of our SharePoint farm to make it ready for end users.

CHAPTER 6

Scaling the Farm Using Terraform and Ansible

In the previous two chapters, we walked you through deploying our farm to Azure and AWS using Infrastructure as Code. We then performed configuration management using Ansible to install SharePoint based on our topology.

In this chapter, we go through the exercise of scaling the Azure SharePoint farm topology discussed in Chapter 4 by making the WFE role highly available using Azure availability sets. We use Terraform to specify the objects. We also add a load balancer to distribute incoming traffic.

Farm Topology

We will modify the previous farm topology to make the role highly available. Figure 6-1 shows what the architecture will look like. We are also adding an Azure load balancer to control traffic to our WFEs.

© Oscar Medina, Ethan Schumann 2018
O. Medina and E. Schumann, *DevOps for SharePoint*, https://doi.org/10.1007/978-1-4842-3688-8_6

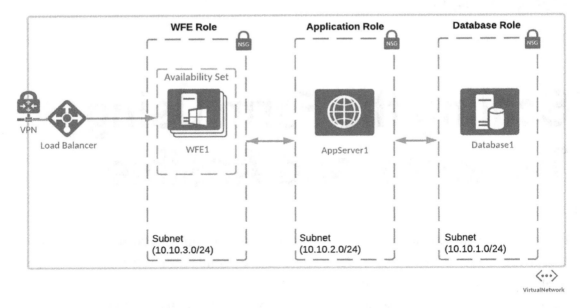

Figure 6-1. *The SharePoint 2016 farm using Azure availability sets for the WFE role*

Architecture Changes

There are several architectural changes that we will walk through in this chapter to help you understand how to scale a SharePoint farm rapidly and in a repeatable, predictable fashion. The following includes some of the major changes.

- We add availability sets for the WFE role to make them highly available and redundant.

- We add a load balancer to manage traffic to our WFEs.

- We place each SharePoint role in its respective subnet and NSGs.

- We create a Packer image to quickly spin up additional WFEs. This image has the SharePoint bits and prerequisites installed, which allows us to run an Ansible playbook to add the new WFEs to the farm.

Please note that not all roles are made highly available for this walkthrough. The aim of this chapter is to show you how to do this for a given tier; in this case, the *web front end* role, using Terraform, Ansible, and Packer.

> **Note**   We focus on the scaling the Azure cloud farm we deployed in earlier chapters. However, the code can be enhanced (and perhaps this is a good challenge for you) to scale the AWS SharePoint 2016 farm deployment by modifying the Terraform IaC.

Building the Packer WFE Image

Earlier chapters showed you how to create a Packer Windows 2016 server image as a base image for the SharePoint 2016 farm. We had a vanilla OS with a VSCode and a couple of other software packages. However, another approach is to create an image per SharePoint role, which is preloaded with the SharePoint prerequisites installed. Using this approach, you can easily join it to the farm. In our case, we want to create an image for the WFE role. Let's go through what you need to do next.

Getting Started

To start creating our Packer template, we copied our existing one and made modifications. The key difference is that we are using the Ansible provisioner to execute our WFE Ansible playbook, which we have also modified. We will go over changes shortly. Once the image is built, it is stored in our storage account, and we will reference this image URL via Terraform at a later time.

The WFE Packer Template

Our new template resides in the following project location: `Packer/azure_windows2016_wfe.json`. We added the Ansible provisioner shown in bold in Listing 6-1. The goal is to preinstall SharePoint 2016 prerequisites on this image, so that at a later time, we simply run the WFE playbook to join it to the domain and add it to the farm.

Listing 6-1. WFE Packer Template Using Ansible Provisioner to Preinstall
SharePoint Prerequisites

```
{
 "variables": {},

  "builders": [{
    "type": "azure-arm",

    "client_id": "",
    "client_secret": "",
    "object_id": "",
    "subscription_id": "",
    "tenant_id": "",
    "resource_group_name": "spfarmstaging",
    "storage_account": "spfarmstaging",

    "capture_container_name": "spfarmstaging",
    "capture_name_prefix": "packer",

    "os_type": "Windows",
    "image_publisher": "MicrosoftWindowsServer",
    "image_offer": "WindowsServer",
    "image_sku": "2016-Datacenter",

    "communicator": "winrm",
    "winrm_use_ssl": "true",
    "winrm_insecure": "true",
    "winrm_timeout": "15m",
    "winrm_username": "packer",

    "azure_tags": {
        "Role": "WFE"
    },

    "location": "West US",
    "vm_size": "Standard_DS2_v2"
  }],
    "provisioners": [
```

```
    {
  "type": "windows-shell",
  "execute_command": "{{ .Vars }} cmd /c \"{{ .Path }}\"",
  "scripts": [
    "scripts/enable-rdp.bat",
    "scripts/chocolatey.bat",
    "scripts/chocopacks.bat"
  ]
},
{
  "type": "windows-shell",
  "execute_command": "{{ .Vars }} cmd /c \"{{ .Path }}\"",
  "scripts": ["scripts/pin-powershell.bat","scripts/set-winrm-
  automatic.bat"]
},
{
  "type": "powershell",
  "scripts": [
    "scripts/disable-screensaver.ps1",
    "scripts/postInstall.ps1",
    "scripts/enable-winrm.ps1"
  ]
},
{
  "type": "ansible",
  "playbook_file": "../ansible/plays/webservers.yml",
  "ansible_env_vars": ["ANSIBLE_CONFIG=../ansible.cfg"],
  "groups":["Webservers"],
  "user": "packer",
  "extra_arguments": [
    "--connection", "packer",
    "--tags=never",
    "--extra-vars", "ansible_shell_type=powershell ansible_shell_
    executable=None cloud_host=Webservers ansible_user=packer",
    "-vvvvv"
  ]
```

```
    },
    {
      "type": "windows-restart",
      "restart_check_command": "powershell -command \"& {Write-Output
      'packer restarted this machine successfully.'}\""
    },
    {
        "type": "powershell",
        "inline": [
            "& $env:SystemRoot\\System32\\Sysprep\\Sysprep.exe /oobe
            /generalize /quiet /quit",
            "while($true) { $imageState = Get-ItemProperty HKLM:\\
            SOFTWARE\\Microsoft\\Windows\\CurrentVersion\\Setup\\State
            | Select ImageState; if($imageState.ImageState -ne 'IMAGE_
            STATE_GENERALIZE_RESEAL_TO_OOBE') { Write-Output $imageState.
            ImageState; Start-Sleep -s 10  } else { break } }"
        ]
    }

  ]
}
```

The Ansible WFE Playbook Changes

As you may have noticed, we are using the same Ansible playbook as we did in earlier chapters. However, a change we made to this playbook, is to include an additional file located at Ansible/roles/WFE/tasks/packer-bootstrap.yml, which contains several tasks which themselves install necessary software such as the utility PSExec, SharePoint 2016 bits. We then download the SharePoint prerequisites and install them on this image.

The playbook also copies the folder structure we created in our GitHub repository as per the SPAutoInstaller structure and drops the downloaded prerequisites in the respective folder. We then install the SharePoint prerequisites and mount the SharePoint image to extract it into the SPAutoInstaller folder as well.

Listing 6-2. The Ansible Tasks Used By Packer to Bootstrap the WFE Image

```
- name: Install PSExec
  win_chocolatey:
    name: psexec
  ignore_errors: yes
  tags:
    - never

- name: Download SharePoint 2016
  win_get_url:
    url: https://download.microsoft.com/download/0/0/4/004EE264-7043-45BF-
    99E3-3F74ECAE13E5/officeserver.img
    dest: c:\
    force: no
  tags:
    - never

# This task mounts the Officeserver.img file
- name: Mount the SharePoint Bits IMG
  win_disk_image:
      image_path: c:\officeserver.img
      state: present
  register: disk_image_out
  tags:
    - never

- name: Create c:\SP directory
  win_file:
    path: C:\SP
    state: directory
  tags:
    - never

- name: Copy SP folder (SPAutoInstaller folder structure)
  win_copy:
    src: ../../common/files/SP/
    dest: C:\SP
```

```
      force: false
    tags:
      - never

  - name: Copy SP Prerequisites Downloader PowerShell Script
    win_copy:
      src: ../../common/files/DownloadPrerequisites.ps1
      dest: C:\SP\DownloadPrerequisites.ps1
      force: false
    tags:
      - never

  - name: Copy SP Prerequisites Installer PowerShell Script
    win_copy:
      src: ../../common/files/Install-Prerequisites.ps1
      dest: C:\SP\Install-Prerequisites.ps1
      force: false
    tags:
      - never

  - name: Copy SP Bits in {{ disk_image_out.mount_path }} to SPAutoInstaller
    folder structure
    win_shell: XCOPY {{ disk_image_out.mount_path }}\* C:\SP\2016\SharePoint\
    /s /i /Y
    args:
    executable: cmd
    tags:
      - never

  - name: Download SharePoint Prerequisites
    win_shell: C:\SP\DownloadPrerequisites.ps1 -SPPrerequisitesPath c:\
    SP\2016\prerequisiteinstallerfiles
    tags:
      - never

  - name: Install SharePoint Prerequisites via PowerShell
    win_shell: C:\SP\Install-Prerequisites.ps1 -SharePointBitsPath c:\
    SP\2016\SharePoint
```

```
tags:
  - never

- name: Install All Required Windows Features
  win_feature:
    name: NET-HTTP-Activation,NET-Non-HTTP-Activ,NET-WCF-Pipe-
    Activation45,NET-WCF-HTTP-Activation45,Web-Server,Web-WebServer,Web-
    Common-Http,Web-Static-Content,Web-Default-Doc,Web-Dir-Browsing,Web-
    Http-Errors,Web-App-Dev,Web-Asp-Net,Web-Asp-Net45,Web-Net-Ext,Web-
    Net-Ext45,Web-ISAPI-Ext,Web-ISAPI-Filter,Web-Health,Web-Http-
    Logging,Web-Log-Libraries,Web-Request-Monitor,Web-Http-Tracing,Web-
    Security,Web-Basic-Auth,Web-Windows-Auth,Web-Filtering,Web-Digest-
    Auth,Web-Performance,Web-Stat-Compression,Web-Dyn-Compression,Web-Mgmt-
    Tools,Web-Mgmt-Console,Web-Mgmt-Compat,Web-Metabase,WAS,WAS-Process-
    Model,WAS-NET-Environment,WAS-Config-APIs,Web-Lgcy-Scripting,Windows-
    Identity-Foundation,Xps-Viewer
    state: present
    restart: yes
    include_sub_features: yes
    include_management_tools: yes
  register: feature_result
  tags:
    - never
```

> **Tip** You might have noticed that each task has a tag with the **–never** value. This tag is available as of Ansible 2.5, so we can use this tag to exclude specific tasks when running the playbook. More information is at `http://docs.ansible.com/ansible/latest/user_guide/playbooks_tags.html`.

In addition, you can also specify to only run the tasks with the tag, as shown in our Packer template in Listing 6-1.

To build the image we simply run the following command from within the Packer folder as follows.

```
>$ Packer build azure_win2016_wfe.json
```

Once the task completes, it will output the VHD URL that we will use in our Terraform definition in the next section.

Scaling Farm Topology Using Terraform

When it comes to scaling any application on the cloud, we have many options at our disposal. We have to make decisions in how we approach this and leverage native cloud services and features as much as possible is one of those conundrums we face constantly.

In the traditional data center, we add additional servers to an n-tier application; whereas in the cloud, we add virtual machines and leverage other capabilities. For Azure, its virtual machine availability sets. For SharePoint deployments, we typically find ourselves adding VMs for a specific role.

In this chapter, we show you how to leverage Azure features that help scale and make your SharePoint farm highly available. We will use Terraform to describe Azure resources as we have been, but we will make several changes as outlined in the "Architecture Changes" section.

Scaling Up

Scaling up, or vertically, means that we need to add more resources to our virtual machines. For example, our WFEs may need more CPU, RAM, and so forth, to meet SLAs. To quickly do this, we can modify the definition of our Terraform VMs and specify an Azure VM size. We previously defined our WFE in Terraform, the property we would modify is called vm_size. We specify a different size as per Azure available sizes.

Listing 6-3. VM Size Property to Change to Scale up the VMs That Are Used for the WFE Role

```
resource "azurerm_virtual_machine" "spfarm_wfe" {

    name                  = "spfarm_wfe"
    location              = "West US"
    resource_group_name   = "${var.resource_group_name}"
    vm_size               = "Standard_DS2_v2"
    network_interface_ids = ["${azurerm_network_interface.spfarm-wfe.id}"]
    availability_set_id   = "${azurerm_availability_set.WebFrontEnd_
    AvailabilitySet.id}"
```

```
  storage_os_disk {
    name            = "WFE1-osdisk1"
    os_type         = "Windows"
    caching         = "ReadWrite"
    image_uri       = "${var.os_disk_vhd_uri}"
    vhd_uri         = "https://${var.storage_account}.blob.core.windows.
                       net/${var.container_name}/wfe1-osdisk.vhd"
    create_option = "FromImage"
  }

  os_profile {
    computer_name   = "SP2016WFE"
    admin_username = "packer"
    admin_password = "pass@word1!"
  }

  os_profile_windows_config {
        provision_vm_agent = true
        enable_automatic_upgrades = true
  }

  provisioner "remote-exec" {
    connection = {
      type        = "winrm"
      user        = "packer"
      password    = "pass@word1!"
      agent       = "false"
      host        = "${azurerm_public_ip.wfe1-public-ip.ip_address}"
    }
    inline = ["powershell.exe Set-ExecutionPolicy RemoteSigned -force",
    "powershell.exe -version 4 -ExecutionPolicy Bypass Restart-Computer"]
  }
}
```

To make the change to this virtual machine, we execute the following command.

```
>$ terraform apply –var-file terraform.tfvars
```

Note that in this scenario, all that happens is that the actual Azure virtual machine size is changed as desired, and the OS disk we are using remains intact. This means that we still have our SharePoint bits installed and the machine is still joined to our SharePoint farm.

Tip   For most enterprise environments, cost savings are a major focus, especially when it comes to cloud usage. If you notice that certain machines are not being used frequently, you can easily scale down by changing this property to a smaller size, given the availability of other sizes in the cluster that the existing VM is in.

Scaling Out

Scaling out, or horizontally, means that we add WFEs for our front end, for example. We will define additional WFEs in our Terraform definition, and then run Ansible to run the SharePoint installer. We will then deploy both WFEs within a virtual machine availability set, which itself is receiving traffic from a public load balancer (shown in Figure 6-1).

About Virtual Machine Availability Sets

Azure virtual machine availability sets bring availability and reliability for our virtual machines. availability sets are a logical grouping in Azure that when used, isolate our virtual machines from each other. The machines are deployed across different nodes and cluster. Should a hardware failure occur in Azure, not all of the virtual machines would be affected.

For our SharePoint farm, we place each the WebFrontEnd role into an availability set and add at least two virtual machines to ensure that we are covered by higher service level agreement (SLA).

Terraforming Multiple WFE Virtual Machines

In Chapter 4, we defined our core networking resources and our virtual machines as we prepared to deploy our SharePoint farm to Azure. We declared a single virtual machine for each role, however. In order to scale our farm, we need to add WFEs. To do this, we want to change the way we declare our virtual machines and network interfaces.

Changing the Network Interface Declaration

The file we modify is located at `terraform/azure/environments/staging/network.tf`. We continue to leverage Terraform's powerful interpolation by declaring our network interface as follows. Notice we have a `count` property declared as well. The network interface `name` property also uses the `count.index` to append the value to have a unique name for these network interface cards.

Listing 6-4. Declaring Multiple Network Interfaces in Terraform

```
resource "azurerm_network_interface" "spfarm-wfe" {
  count                           = 2
  name                            = "network-interface-spfarm-
                                    wfe${count.index}"
  location                        = "${var.location}"
  resource_group_name             = "${var.resource_group_name}"
  network_security_group_id       = "${azurerm_network_security_
                                    group.spfarm-security-group-
                                    frontend.id}"
  dns_servers                     = ["10.10.1.19"]

  ip_configuration {
    name                          = "wfe${count.index}-ipconfiguration"
    subnet_id                     = "${azurerm_subnet.subnet-frontend.id}"
    private_ip_address_allocation = "dynamic"
    load_balancer_backend_address_pools_ids = ["${azurerm_lb_backend_
                                               address_pool.bpepool.id}"]
  }

  tags {
   environment = "Staging"
  }
}
```

Note   The network interfaces do not use public IP addresses as we want to use our public load balancer to accept traffic for our WFE, hence declaring the load_balancer_backend_pools_ids property within our ip_configuration block.

Declaring the Virtual Machine Availability Set

Declaring a virtual machine availability set in Terraform is actually quite simple. The key is to add virtual machines to it when declaring them in Terraform, as we will do shortly.

Listing 6-5. Terraform Virtual Machine Availability Set Declaration

```
resource "azurerm_availability_set" "WebFrontEnd_AvailabilitySet" {

    name                          = "WebFrontEnd_AvailabilitySet"
    location                      = "${var.location}"
    resource_group_name           = "${var.resource_group_name}"
    platform_fault_domain_count   = 2
    platform_update_domain_count  = 2
    managed                       = false

}
```

When adding VMs to an availability set, Azure automatically assigns each VM an *update domain* and a *fault domain*. By default, availability sets have two fault domains, each sharing a common power source and network switch, and VMs are automatically separated across the fault domains.

Modifying the WFE VM Terraform Declaration

We must declare at least two WFEs to add them to the availability set. Terraform allows us to do this easily with its powerful meta-parameter called count and interpolation capabilities. We add the count property and indicate the number of WFEs that should be created, as shown next.

Tip   Count is part of Terraform meta-parameters available to us. For more information, visit www.terraform.io/docs/configuration/resources.html#count.

In addition to indicating the number of WFEs, we want to make sure the name of our virtual machine is unique, so we use the count index to append it to the name property (shown in bold in Listing 6-6). We ensure our WFEs are part of the availability set by setting the value of the availability_set_id property value.

Listing 6-6. Declaring Multiple Virtual Machines in Terraform for the WFE Role

```
resource "azurerm_virtual_machine" "spfarm_wfe" {

  count                   = 2
  name                    = "SP2016WFE${count.index}"
  location                = "${var.location}"
  resource_group_name     = "${var.resource_group_name}"
  vm_size                 = "Standard_DS2_v2"

  network_interface_ids = ["${element(azurerm_network_interface.spfarm-
  wfe.*.id, count.index)}"]
  availability_set_id     = "${azurerm_availability_set.WebFrontEnd_
                            AvailabilitySet.id}"

# Uncomment this line to delete the OS disk automatically when deleting
the VM
# delete_os_disk_on_termination = true

# Uncomment this line to delete the data disks automatically when deleting
the VM delete_data_disks_on_termination = true

  storage_os_disk {
    name         = "WFE${count.index}-osdisk1"
    os_type      = "Windows"
    caching      = "ReadWrite"
    image_uri    = "${var.os_disk_wfe_vhd_uri}"
    vhd_uri      = "https://${var.storage_account}.blob.core.windows.
                    net/${var.container_name}/wfe${count.index}-osdisk.vhd"
    create_option = "FromImage"
  }

  os_profile {
    computer_name  = "SP2016WFE${count.index}"
    admin_username = "packer"
    admin_password = "pass@word1!"
  }
```

```
os_profile_windows_config {
      provision_vm_agent = true
      enable_automatic_upgrades = true
  }

}
```

Earlier in this chapter, we built the WFE role–specific Packer image. It is time for us to use it. We ensure that the `image_uri` within our virtual machine declaration contains the blob URL where we stored the image. To make things easier, we declare another variable within our `variables.tf` called `os_disk_wfe_vhd_uri`, which contains the full blob URL of our packer image VHD. We then use that variable as the value of the `image_url` property.

Terraforming the Load Balancer and NAT Rules

Now that our WFEs are deployed within a virtual machine availability set, we need to point traffic to this availability set. To do this, it is a best practice to use a load balancer. We declare a public load balancer and related artifacts including probes, public IP, and basic load balancing rules.

The contents of our file located at `terraform/azure/environments/staging/loadbalancer.tf` should look similar to the Listing 6-7.

Listing 6-7. Load Balancer and Related Artifacts

```
# Load Balancers and associated pools
resource "azurerm_lb" "WebFrontEnd_LB" {
  name                = "WebFrontEnd_LB"
  location            = "${var.location}"
  resource_group_name = "${var.resource_group_name}"

  frontend_ip_configuration {
    name                         = "Web-LB-FrontEnd"
    public_ip_address_id         = "${azurerm_public_ip.webfrontend-lb-
                                      public-ip.id}"

  }

}
```

```
resource "azurerm_public_ip" "webfrontend-lb-public-ip" {
  name                         = "webfrontend-lb-public-ip"
  location                     = "${var.location}"
  resource_group_name          = "${var.resource_group_name}"
  public_ip_address_allocation = "static"

  tags {
    environment = "SharePoint 2016 Staging"
  }
}

resource "azurerm_lb_backend_address_pool" "bpepool" {
  resource_group_name = "${var.resource_group_name}"
  loadbalancer_id     = "${azurerm_lb.WebFrontEnd_LB.id}"
  name                = "Web-LB-BackendPool"
}
resource "azurerm_lb_nat_pool" "lbnatpool" {
  count                          = 2
  resource_group_name            = "${var.resource_group_name}"
  name                           = "ssh"
  loadbalancer_id                = "${azurerm_lb.WebFrontEnd_LB.id}"
  protocol                       = "Tcp"
  frontend_port_start            = 50000
  frontend_port_end              = 50119
  backend_port                   = 22
  frontend_ip_configuration_name = "Web-LB-FrontEnd"

}

# LB Probes
resource "azurerm_lb_probe" "lbprobe443" {
  resource_group_name = "${var.resource_group_name}"
  loadbalancer_id     = "${azurerm_lb.WebFrontEnd_LB.id}"
  name                = "lbprobe443"
  port                = 443

}
```

```
resource "azurerm_lb_probe" "lbprobe80" {
  resource_group_name = "${var.resource_group_name}"
  loadbalancer_id     = "${azurerm_lb.WebFrontEnd_LB.id}"
  name                = "lbprobe80"
  port                = 80
}
resource "azurerm_lb_probe" "lbprobe3389" {
  resource_group_name = "${var.resource_group_name}"
  loadbalancer_id     = "${azurerm_lb.WebFrontEnd_LB.id}"
  name                = "lbprob3389"https://www.terraform.io/docs/
                        providers/azurerm/d/image.html
  port                = 3389
}

# LB Rules
resource "azurerm_lb_rule" "lbrule443" {
  resource_group_name              = "${var.resource_group_name}"
  loadbalancer_id                  = "${azurerm_lb.WebFrontEnd_LB.id}"
  name                             = "lbrule"
  protocol                         = "Tcp"
  frontend_port                    = 443
  backend_port                     = 443
  backend_address_pool_id          = "${azurerm_lb_backend_address_pool.
                                       bpepool.id}"
  probe_id                         = "${azurerm_lb_probe.lbprobe443.id}"
  frontend_ip_configuration_name = "Web-LB-FrontEnd"

}
resource "azurerm_lb_rule" "lbrule80" {
  resource_group_name              = "${var.resource_group_name}"
  loadbalancer_id                  = "${azurerm_lb.WebFrontEnd_LB.id}"
  name                             = "lbrule80"
  protocol                         = "Tcp"
  frontend_port                    = 80
  backend_port                     = 80
  backend_address_pool_id          = "${azurerm_lb_backend_address_pool.
                                       bpepool.id}"
```

```
  probe_id                          = "${azurerm_lb_probe.lbprobe80.id}"
  frontend_ip_configuration_name = "Web-LB-FrontEnd"

}
resource "azurerm_lb_rule" "lbrule3389" {
  resource_group_name               = "${var.resource_group_name}"
  loadbalancer_id                   = "${azurerm_lb.WebFrontEnd_LB.id}"
  name                              = "lbrule80"
  protocol                          = "Tcp"
  frontend_port                     = 3389
  backend_port                      = 3389
  backend_address_pool_id           = "${azurerm_lb_backend_address_pool.
                                        bpepool.id}"
  probe_id                          = "${azurerm_lb_probe.lbprobe3389.id}"
  frontend_ip_configuration_name = "Web-LB-FrontEnd"

}


# NAT Rules to allow access to each VM
resource "azurerm_lb_nat_rule" "NatRule0" {
  name                              = "NatRule-${count.index}"
  resource_group_name               = "${var.resource_group_name}"
  loadbalancer_id                   = "${azurerm_lb.WebFrontEnd_LB.id}"
  protocol                          = "tcp"
  frontend_port                     = "5985${count.index + 1}"
  backend_port                      = 5985
  frontend_ip_configuration_name = "Web-LB-FrontEnd"
  count                             = 2
  depends_on                        = ["azurerm_lb.WebFrontEnd_LB"]
}
```

Tip Accessing availability set Nodes is typically done using a bastion or jump box, and you should certainly follow this practice. However, for our example, we will take a simple approach and access an individual machine from the virtual machine availability set by configuring inbound NAT rules.

We configure a single NAT rule on the load balancer to allow Ansible to execute the playbooks. This happens via port 5985, which is the back-end port, as shown in Listing 6-8. The front-end port ends up being different for each VM. For example, for the WFE0, the NAT rule front-end port is 59851 and the WFE1 is 59852 (see `www.terraform.io/docs/providers/azurerm/d/image.html`).

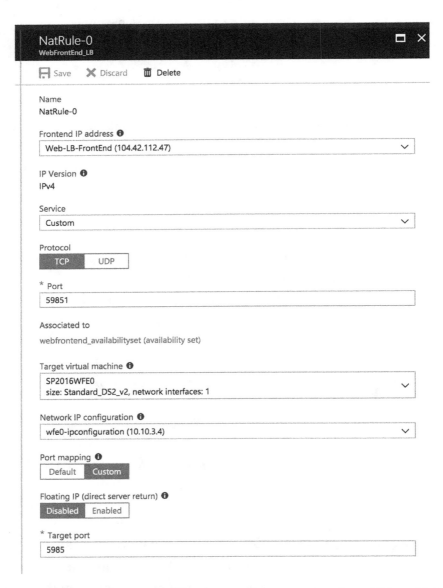

Figure 6-2. *Load balancer NAT rule shows port mapping for WFE0 within our availability set*

Provisioning the New SharePoint 2016 Farm

Now that we have made all the changes to our Terraform code, it is time to provision our site to Azure. But first, let's take a look at what will be provisioned. To do that, we execute the following command (this should be familiar to you at this point).

```
>$ terraform plan
```

The output in Listing 6-8 is trimmed for brevity. However, we want to show you the two WFEs that Terraform will provision given our new declaration.

Listing 6-8. The two WFEs Added to the Availability Set

```
+ azurerm_virtual_machine.spfarm_wfe[0]
      id:                                                <computed>
      availability_set_id:                               "${azurerm_
                                                         availability_set.
                                                         webfrontend_avail-
                                                         abilityset.id}"

      delete_data_disks_on_termination:                  "true"
      delete_os_disk_on_termination:                     "false"
      identity.#:                                        <computed>
      location:                                          "westus"
      name:                                              "SP2016WFE0"
      network_interface_ids.#:                           <computed>
      os_profile.#:                                      "1"
      os_profile.1539969592.admin_password:              <sensitive>
      os_profile.1539969592.admin_username:              "packer"
      os_profile.1539969592.computer_name:               "SP2016WFE0"
      os_profile.1539969592.custom_data:                 <computed>
      os_profile_windows_config.#:                       "1"
      os_profile_windows_config.2256145325.additional_
      unattend_config.#:                                 "0"
      os_profile_windows_config.2256145325.enable_
      automatic_upgrades:                                "true"
      os_profile_windows_config.2256145325.provision_
      vm_agent:                                          "true"
```

```
    os_profile_windows_config.2256145325.winrm.#:    "0"
    resource_group_name:                             "spfarmstaging"
    storage_image_reference.#:                       <computed>
    storage_os_disk.#:                               "1"
    storage_os_disk.0.caching:                       "ReadWrite"
    storage_os_disk.0.create_option:                 "FromImage"
    storage_os_disk.0.disk_size_gb:                  <computed>
    storage_os_disk.0.image_uri:                     "https://spfarms-
                                                     taging.blob.core.
                                                     windows.net/system/
                                                     Microsoft.Compute/
                                                     Images/spfarmstaging/
                                                     packer-osDisk.
                                                     5fd747c3-2933-4f09-
                                                     af1e-12bf65d1c476.vhd"
    storage_os_disk.0.managed_disk_id:               <computed>
    storage_os_disk.0.managed_disk_type:             <computed>
    storage_os_disk.0.name:                          "WFE0-osdisk1"
    storage_os_disk.0.os_type:                       "Windows"
    storage_os_disk.0.vhd_uri:                       "https://spfarms-
                                                     taging.blob.core.
                                                     windows.net/
                                                     spfarmstaging/
                                                     wfe0-osdisk.vhd"
    tags.%:                                          <computed>
    vm_size:                                         "Standard_DS2_v2"

+ azurerm_virtual_machine.spfarm_wfe[1]
    id:                                              <computed>
    availability_set_id:                             "${azurerm_
                                                     availability_
                                                     set.webfrontend_
                                                     availabilityset.
                                                     id}"
```

```
delete_data_disks_on_termination:                        "true"
delete_os_disk_on_termination:                           "false"
identity.#:                                              <computed>
location:                                                "westus"
name:                                                    "SP2016WFE1"
network_interface_ids.#:                                <computed>
os_profile.#:                                            "1"
os_profile.1121002361.admin_password:                    <sensitive>
os_profile.1121002361.admin_username:                    "packer"
os_profile.1121002361.computer_name:                     "SP2016WFE1"
os_profile.1121002361.custom_data:                       <computed>
os_profile_windows_config.#:                             "1"
os_profile_windows_config.2256145325.additional_
unattend_config.#:                                       "0"
os_profile_windows_config.2256145325.enable_
automatic_upgrades:                                      "true"
os_profile_windows_config.2256145325.provision_
vm_agent:                                                "true"
os_profile_windows_config.2256145325.winrm.#:            "0"
resource_group_name:                                     "spfarmstaging"
storage_image_reference.#:                              <computed>
storage_os_disk.#:                                       "1"
storage_os_disk.0.caching:                               "ReadWrite"
storage_os_disk.0.create_option:                         "FromImage"
storage_os_disk.0.disk_size_gb:                         <computed>
storage_os_disk.0.image_uri:                             "https://spfarmst-
                                                         aging.blob.core.
                                                         windows.net/
                                                         system/Microsoft.
                                                         Compute/Images/
                                                         spfarmstaging/
                                                         packer-osDisk.
                                                         5fd747c3-2933-4f09-
                                                         af1e-12bf65d1c476.vhd"
storage_os_disk.0.managed_disk_id:                          <computed>
```

storage_os_disk.0.managed_disk_type:	\<computed\>
storage_os_disk.0.name:	**"WFE1-osdisk1"**
storage_os_disk.0.os_type:	"Windows"
storage_os_disk.0.vhd_uri:	"https://spfarmst- aging.blob.core. windows.net/ spfarmstaging/ wfe1-osdisk.vhd"
tags.%:	\<computed\>
vm_size:	"Standard_DS2_v2"

Once we are happy with the output of the plan, we simply execute the following command to provision it all.

```
>$ terraform apply –var-file=terraform.tfvars
```

Performing Configuration Management on the WFEs

Earlier in this chapter, we walked through the changes needed for the provisioning aspect of our WFEs in order to scale our farm. We now have them provisioned in Azure, but we are not done.

We now need to access each one of them and finish installing the SharePoint bits. Then, we join the machine to the SharePoint 2016 farm.

Accessing the WFEs in the Availability Set

To access our WFEs, which are now behind a load balancer, we temporarily add a public IP (PIP) to each VM, which in our case is WFE0 and WFE1, respectively.

Caution   We do this to run the one-time Ansible configuration management. We remove the PIPs once we finish the configuration, as we do not want to have them accessed, but rather use the load balancer to receive incoming traffic for our availability set. In a production environment, you might opt to run Ansible via a VM in Azure. Using the Azure Shell is another great alternative.

For each VM, go to the Azure portal and associate the corresponding PIP. Our Terraform code provisioned them, but we intentionally left the PIPs disassociated. Once you have each WFE with a temporary public IP, you are ready to run the Ansible playbooks to finish installing SharePoint and then join them to the farm.

Joining WFEs to the SharePoint Farm

Our WFE Ansible playbook has been modified. We've created an additional task file located at `Ansible/roles/internal/WFE/tasks/join-server-to-farm.yml`, which contains the tasks we must run to join the WFE to the farm. The playbook is shown in Listing 6-9.

Listing 6-9. The Playbook Tasks to Join the WFE1 to the Existing Farm

```
- name: Copy addServerToFarm PowerShell Script
  win_copy:
    src: ../../common/files/addServerToFarm.ps1
    dest: C:\SP\addServerToFarm.ps1
    force: false
  tags:
  - join-to-farm

- name: Trigger AutoSPInstaller (computer will restart and continue install)
  win_psexec:
    command: C:\SP\AutoSPInstaller\AutoSPInstallerLaunch.bat
    priority: high
    elevated: yes
    interactive: yes
    username: sposcar\vagrant
    password: Pass@word1!
    wait: no
  tags:
  - join-to-farm

- name: wait 300 seconds for port 2016 to become open on the host, don't
start checking for 60 seconds
```

```
  win_wait_for:
    port: 2016
    host: {{cloud_host}}
    state: started
    delay: 60
  tags:
  - join-to-farm

- name: Join Server to existing SharePoint 2016 Farm
  win_psexec:
    command: powershell.exe Start-Process "$PSHOME\powershell.exe"
-ArgumentList "'-NoExit -ExecutionPolicy Bypass  C:\SP\addServerToFarm.
ps1 -DBServer SP2016SQLSERVER -DBName DEV_Config -PassPhrase Pass@word1!
-SP2016 -ServerRole WebFrontEnd'"
    priority: high
    elevated: yes
    interactive: yes
    username: sposcar\vagrant
    password: Pass@word1!
    wait: no
  tags:
  - join-to-farm
```

Tip   Please note that for our examples code, we do not always use variables within our Ansible playbooks, but it is certainly a best practice and helps code maintainability. Items like the usernames and passwords in Listing 6-9 are good candidates for this and would be placed in the ansible/group_vars/all.yml file.

We execute the following command.

```
>$ ansible-playbook -i ansible/azure_rm.py ansible/plays/webservers.
yml --extra-vars="cloud_host='SP2016WFE1' ansible_user='packer' ansible_
password='pass@word1!'" –tags="join-to-domain,join-to-farm" -vvvv
```

We are instructing Ansible to execute our WFE playbook, but in addition to that, make sure that it only executes the tasks with the tags specified. This is because we want to make sure that server is joined to our sposcar.local domain, and we need to join the WFE to the farm with the `WebFrontEnd` role.

At this point, we have a full farm deployed and configured in Azure. There is a lot of room to improve our configuration management, and we encourage you to make use of the GitHub repository as a starting point to provision and manage your farms, in the cloud or on-premises.

One of the major areas to be cautious about and improve upon is the passwords that are used across the solution. Using HashiCorp Vault would be a great addition to manage these passwords and encrypt them; examples are at `https://docs.ansible.com/ ansible/latest/plugins/lookup/hashi_vault.html`.

Another aspect of the code that needs improvement is using WinRM via port 5986 by default for encrypted traffic; this is a little more work, as it requires certificates, but it is certainly worthwhile to implement. Ansible also has built-in secret protection via Ansible Vault.

In addition, since we have our IaC in GitHub, we can use CI/CD pipelines to test our changes, which is typical of the developer workflow.

Summary

In this chapter, we walked through how to scale the SharePoint 2016 farm using Terraform's interpolation capabilities and leveraging Azure availability sets. We showed you how you can build a Packer image for a given role in the farm. In our scenario, we created an image for the WFE role, which we prepopulated with the SharePoint prerequisites and installed them on the image. We did this using the Ansible Packer provisioner. You can easily do this for the application server role using this technique.

## CHAPTER 7

Establishing an Enterprise Environment to Manage and Collaborate as a Team

While the previous chapters focused on the technical configurations of deploying a SharePoint farm using modern tooling and practices, it is important to be able manage these processes at an enterprise level. Proper access control, automation, and workflow are instrumental in ensuring that these practices can scale and meet the demand of an ever-changing organization. Following are some industry standards and best practices that can enable your team and organization.

Version Control

While you are undoubtedly familiar with version control (we did use it in our previous chapters after all), it is worth briefly mentioning the core concepts and advantages of using it. Version control is not a new technology and has in fact grown over the past decades via various implementations. The concept is simple; keep your code in a single place that is considered the single "version of truth" for your environment. Traditionally this has been utilized to manage application code. With the inception of concepts such as configuration management and IaC, we can now leverage version control to maintain, develop, and test not only applications but infrastructure and the complex configurations of enterprise environments.

While the code used in this book is in GitHub, there are various products that implement the same branch-based control mechanisms such as GitLab and Bitbucket, and while there are some differences, none is drastic enough to warrant specific consideration.

O. Medina and E. Schumann, *DevOps for SharePoint*, https://doi.org/10.1007/978-1-4842-3688-8_7

Orchestration

Orchestration is the practice of using automation tooling to implement predictable and repeatable workflows for effecting changes in your environment. For the purposes of this book we will focus on the creation and maintenance of infrastructure, not addressing other activities commonly addressed by orchestration (code compilation, artifact creation, etc.). There are several products in this space that offer a dichotomy of practices and philosophies on how to orchestrate your environment. While these differences exist and should be considered when selecting a tool, the concept of using them for automating your environment remains largely the same. As such, we will focus on the *what* as opposed to the *how*.

Whatever the tool, the goal is the same. Utilizing an automation platform will allow you to script the workflows necessary for deploying your infrastructure. This can be written in shell for Linux based automation systems, PowerShell on Windows, or even a proprietary plugin found within the tool. For the purposes of our example we will examine a script used in Jenkins to automate a Terraform deployment. For context, Jenkins allows Automation as Code via a Jenkinsfile, which is a script written in the Groovy programming language that specifies the desired steps to run for a build pipeline, or part of a pipeline. A typical Jenkinsfile contains the various build steps, any parameters that the operator specifies, and usually some basic error handling. The following Jenkinsfile has these basic sections:

- **Agent**. Defines which Jenkins instance to run on. Agent means we will run this job on any available Jenkins master/slave.

- **Parameters**. Input parameters provided by the operator at the beginning of each job. Here we specify the following:

  - TERRAFORM_COMMAND. Performs a Terraform apply or destroy.

  - PROJECT. The name of a project. It is used to create a Terraform workspace, isolating the location of this code on the file system from other projects.

  - PHASE. The environment that is run (i.e., dev, QA, prod).

226

- **Environment.** Here we set some environment variables for the context run. The following variables should be edited; the others are dynamically populated from other parameters in the job.

  - GIT_REPO. The repo to clone. This is where our Terraform code lives.

  - GIT_CREDENTIALS. The ID of an SSH key stored in Jenkins.

  - TF_VARIABLES_FILE. The name of a file to be used if there is a Terraform variables file. If this file does not exist, the pipeline will still execute successfully.

- **Steps**

  - Initialization. Here we check out the Git repo from the master branch so that we can conduct a build.

  - Terraform apply. Here we conduct the following:

    - terraform init. Initializes the workspace; ensures we have all modules needed.

    - terraform workspace. Selects the workspace represented by the PROJECT variable.

    - terraform plan. - A test of the Terraform code is conducted.

    - terraform apply. The Terraform code is executed against our environment.

  - Terraform destroy. Here we conduct the following:

    - terraform workspace. Selects the workspace represented by the PROJECT variable.

    - terraform destroy. Destroys the infrastructure that has been deployed.

```groovy
#!groovy

pipeline {

    agent any

    parameters {
        choice (name: 'TERRAFORM_COMMAND', choices: 'create\ndestroy',
        description: 'Terraform Apply / Destroy.')
```

```
        string (name: 'PROJECT', defaultValue: 'demoProject', description:
        'Specify the project for the deployment.')

        choice (name: 'PHASE', choices: 'dev\nqa\nprod', description:
        'Specify development phase.')

    }

    environment {
        IS_JENKINS_MODE              = "true"
        GIT_REPO                     = "[INSERT GIT REPO TO CLONE]"
        GIT_CREDENTIALS              = "[INSERT JENKINS GIT
                                       CREDENTIALS]"
        TF_STATE_ENV                 = "${params.PROJECT}-${params.
                                       FACTORY}-${params.PHASE}-${params.
                                       VISIBILITY}"
        TF_CONFIG_DIR                = "tf_config_dir"
        TF_VARIABLES_FILE            = "vars.tfvars"
        AWS_TIMEOUT_SECONDS          = 600
    }

    stages {

        stage("Initialization") {
            steps {
                git branch: "develop", changelog: false, credentialsId:
                "${GIT_CREDENTIALS}", poll: false, url: "${GIT_REPO}"

                // Validate that the specified global variables file exists
                for this deployment
                sh "if [ -e ${TF_VARIABLES_FILE} ] ; then echo Found
                Terraform variables file: ${TF_VARIABLES_FILE} ; else echo
                Cannot find Terraform variables file: ${TF_VARIABLES_FILE} ;
                exit 1 ; fi"
            }
        }
```

```
        stage("Terraform Apply") {
            when { expression { params.TERRAFORM_COMMAND == 'create' } }
            steps {
                withEnv(["PATH+TF=${tool 'terraform'}"]) {
                    sh 'echo "Starting Terraform Deployment creation"'
                    sh 'echo "Checking directory"'
                    sh "terraform init -force-copy"
                    sh 'terraform workspace list'
                    sh "[ \$(terraform workspace list | grep -c ${TF_STATE_
                    ENV}) -lt 1 ] && terraform workspace new ${TF_STATE_ENV}
                    || echo found Terraform environment ${TF_STATE_ENV}"
                    sh 'terraform workspace select ${TF_STATE_ENV}'
                    sh "terraform plan -var datestamp=\$(date +%y%m%d%H%M)
                    -var-file=${TF_VARIABLES_FILE}"
                    sh "terraform apply -var datestamp=\$(date +%y%m%d%H%M)
                    -var-file=${TF_VARIABLES_FILE}"
                }
            }
        }

        stage("Terraform Destroy") {
            when { expression { params.TERRAFORM_COMMAND == 'destroy' } }
            steps {
                withEnv(["PATH+TF=${tool 'terraform'}"]) {
                    sh "terraform init"
                    sh 'terraform workspace list'
                    sh 'terraform workspace select ${TF_STATE_ENV}'
                    sh 'terraform show'
                    sh 'terraform destroy -force -var-file=${TF_VARIABLES_
                    FILE} ${extra_var_file}'
                }
            }
        }
    }
}
```

While this Jenkinsfile is generic and doesn't incorporate the complex parameterization that may be required in an enterprise environment (using different branches, automated triggers via webhooks, etc.), it does provide the basic tenets of providing reliable and repeatable automation. Even a basic Jenkinsfile like this describes a workflow for all or part of a set of processes that make up all or part of a build pipeline. It describes expected inputs and outputs and handles logging build information for us. This is a core building block when working in a collaborative environment with several engineers, as this provides us a common set of workflows to develop against. While one engineer may be working on a completely different form of infrastructure as another, both will be aware of the required configuration, directory structure, and so forth, to use. This enforces standardized practices and increases shareability.

Security

If you have ever worked in an enterprise, it is almost guaranteed that the importance and need for mature security practices is at the forefront of the organizations priorities. While automation allows us to abstract the management of security artifacts and user access to code, it comes with its own pitfalls and considerations that must be acknowledged.

Secrets Management

Managing secrets is the practice of abstracting all sensitive authentication and authorization data away from the code base. In the context of IaC and configuration management, this would pertain to things such as SSH keys, username/password combos, authentication tokens, and more. There are several ways to implement secrets management in an organization with various levels of complexity. At a minimum, we want to keep this sensitive data outside of our code base. Storing an SSH key or authentication string in a code base can produce dire results, even if the version control product is only accessible internally.

One enabler of this practice can be to use the orchestration platform of your choice to store secrets. Following our previous Jenkins example, we can store many forms of secrets in the Jenkins encrypted database. This allows us to use common configuration items without storing them locally or within our code. When a job is run, the orchestration platform will handle the injection of these secrets at runtime and secure them once the workflow is completed. Another option would be to make use of Ansible's built-in secret management mechanism, called Ansible Vault and documented at `https://docs.ansible.com/ansible/latest/user_guide/vault.html`.

A more sophisticated implementation would involve extending your secrets management to a secured tool that is designed explicitly for this purpose. A great example is HashiCorp's Vault, which enables the storage and retrieval of secrets via API calls, wherein the secrets are managed in a single place and every usage of any credential is logged for auditing purposes.

Ansible supports integration with HashiCorp's Vault (and other secret management tools) through the use of *lookup plug-ins*, documented at `https://docs.ansible.com/ansible/latest/plugins/lookup.html`.

Access Control

As the great philosopher Uncle Ben from the Spider-Man comics once said, "With great power comes great responsibility." While this is true in life, it is especially apparent in the world of IT. Just because you can, doesn't always mean you *should*. Proper control gates, restriction of access, and logging are critical to ensuring that your environment is secured from bad actors and accidental chaos.

Active Directory has been the de facto standard for role-based access control for decades. It utilizes a centralized storage if users, groups, roles, and policies that dictate who can do what. It is easily extendable across the enterprise via LDAP integration, wherein an application can call Active Directory to see what a user is or isn't allowed to do within the context of that app. We can extend this to our orchestration platform, version control platform, and AWS itself with great effect.

Since we presume that you, the reader, have a basic knowledge of Active Directory, we can focus on what we are securing, not necessarily how. One common example is Ansible Tower, as it can integrate with AD to provide role based access controls. If you have your organization's structure represented in Active Directory groups and roles, you can allow and disallow access to automations via AD group membership.

Code

Controlling who can access what code repositories is a big step in enforcing separation of duties principles and preventing accidental or malicious acts. It is also important to secure the branches that a user is allowed to change. For example, a developer may create code in a feature branch, but should not necessarily be able to push their code to production. Virtually all organizations exercise some form of change control processes which code deployment will be subject to. Allowing only a release manager or team lead to promote code into deployable branches is critical in enforcing only vetted and qualified code is allowed to be deployed.

Automations

Automation is incredibly powerful and inherently dangerous. While it can save countless man hours from performing menial tasks and virtually eliminate human error, automation can also enable a scenario where a single wrong click can have critical impact on a business. To mitigate this risk, any workflows should have limited access/triggers as to when they run. Common practices are to allow only a select group to execute the automations (perhaps via Active Directory integration), or only allow them to be triggered programmatically, such as via a promotion of code to a designated branch. The latter is becoming an increasingly common practice, as it allows the implementation of modern CI/CD practices and removes the need for additional human steps to develop and deploy your infrastructure and configurations.

Environments

Locking down environments is not a new practice, but it is worth mentioning in the context of cloud-based environments. Now that we can rapidly provision and modify the entirety of our IT assets through a management plane, it is more important than ever to control who can access these features. Using the cloud providers built in authorization and authentication methods is mandatory and can also be extended similar to aforementioned Active Directory integrations to enforce centralization of access control in the cloud.

A further consideration is the isolation of environments in different network segments within the cloud. Taking AWS as an example, creating a VPC per environment allows each to be segregated from the other. This prevents accidental cross-environment calls to applications and data stores, limiting the blast radius of any erroneous deployments or bad actors. One caveat to this practice is the need for access to shared resources, such as VPN tunnels, domain controllers, and so forth. This can be enabled by the use of controlled peering between a network segment designated for shared resources, allowing all environments to access a subset of resources.

Resilience

One of the greatest advantages of the cloud is the resilience offered by the geographical distribution of resources. Take advantage of geographical distribution features to prevent downtime for your cloud infrastructure, and ultimately avoid downtime for your applications.

The core philosophy shared by all cloud platforms is to *always plan for failure*. This means for you to assume that your environment will experience an outage, it is just a matter of *when*. With this firmly planted as an organization priority, we can take advantage of the cloud for our SharePoint farm, as well as any and all resources we have.

One Equals Zero

If a single point of failure exists, then we have already failed. We are no longer the minimum viable product for a resource in the cloud, as it invites catastrophe and can be easily avoided. Instead, utilizing proper high availability/disaster recovery techniques such as autoscaling, multiregion deployments, immutability, and a tested failover strategy can make your environment virtually impervious to failure. These practices and features are at the core of what makes cloud-based infrastructure so attractive. You should architect your infrastructure from day one to avoid all single points of failure.

The "Nines" of Availability

By using the aforementioned techniques and practices, major organizations are able to obtain increasingly higher "9's" of availability. This is a metric by which many organizations and services are measured, representing percentage of uptime. For example, a company with four nines of availability has an uptime of 99.99%, equating to only being down only 52.56 minutes per year. Before the invention of publicly accessible cloud providers, obtaining this level of resilience required large amounts of capital expenditure to buy and maintain multiple "copies" of an on-premise or co-located IT infrastructure. This doesn't account for the extra processes need to move data, ensuring network connectivity, and DNS resolution between these traditional datacenters that is greatly reduced by the cloud.

Shared Collaboration

Collaboration is instrumental to maintaining knowledge of the code and systems in use at any organization. Creating an environment where engineers can share, consult each other, and learn from mistakes enables a team to continuously grow and refine technology practices. With that in mind, let's take a look at some of the tools that can make collaboration meaningful and effective.

Terraform Enterprise

While the open source nature of Terraform makes provides an easy point of entry for building IaC, it is worth considering the Terraform Enterprise (TFE) platform to help facilitate team collaboration and provide a common platform to devise and create deployments. On top of the already excellent features provided by the free version of Terraform, Enterprise offers several valuable advantages.

Workspace Management and GUI

The GUI provided by TFE allows teams to have a visual dashboard to create and deploy infrastructure. This enables a "single pane of glass" that your organization can use to provide individual workspaces for each operator. This allows the breaking down of monolithic deployments into discreet components, providing governance and delegation features via fine-grained access controls for various resources. With this capability you can separate the logical components of your infrastructure such as networking, monitoring, and application domains. The existing teams in your organization can now have true separation of duties, allowing only respective teams to deploy the infrastructure they are responsible for.

Version Control Connection

With full integration with your version control provider of choice, infrastructure can be deployed directly based on commits, pull requests (PR), tags, and more. This helps to realize the desire for all infrastructures versioned and represented as desired state; you will know with absolute certainty that the code in your version control repositories reflects exactly what is running in your environment. A key example of how this advantage is realized is via pull requests. When someone submits a pull request/merge request to a branch, TFE does a Terraform plan with the contents of the request and records the results on the PR's page. This helps you avoid merging PRs that cause plan failures.

Secure Variable Management

Variable management can be a challenging task when attempting to control and automate it in a bespoke fashion. With the variable management capabilities of TFE, you can allow teams to reuse various Terraform scripts and modules while securely controlling the variables that are injected into deployments. Some examples of where these features stand out include the ability to customize deployments for various environments with discrete sizes for resources, tagging strategies, and configuration management of the code that gets run against various resources. Additionally, these variables can be set at an enterprise level, so each team working in a different environment is no longer concerned with things such as how big a certain cluster is in dev vs. QA.

Remote Plans, Applies, State Storage, Locking, State Rollback

As you begin deploying increasingly complex infrastructures, having the ability to record any Terraform plan actions and storing them for approval before conducting a deployment provides necessary approval gates to prevent deployment failure. With state storage and locking, you can maintain the state of your environment remotely and prevent multiple overlapping deployments that could result in faulty or undesired infrastructure. Coupled with the state rollback feature, you now have the ability to collaborate and deploy as a team with zero concern for deployment conflicts and an incredibly easy way to rollback deployments to the last good state with the press of a button.

Private Module Registry

Organizations using the Terraform Enterprise module registry can have IT operators serve as experienced "producers," who create the infrastructure templates, and developers or less experienced operators as "consumers," who can easily provision infrastructure following best practices with prebuilt modules. This is a crucial capability so that you can enable your organization to adhere to best practices and desired configurations by putting the most experienced engineers in control of enterprise constructs, while still allowing all operators the freedom to deploy without having to concern themselves with whether they are following best practices.

SaaS Install

TFE provides a cloud-hosted solution for the management of your environment, removing the burden of having to deploy, configure, and maintain your own implementation of Terraform Enterprise. SaaS provides many benefits, such as managing upgrades of your platform, high availability, and failover for the TFE implementation. While many organizations prefer to roll their own tooling and platforms, the flexibility that this provides can be key for an enterprise of any size to have full confidence that such a critical tool is always available with the latest features and capabilities.

Summary

In this chapter, we examined how the concepts and practices covered in previous chapters can be effectively applied at scale in an enterprise environment. This is critical for the successful adoption of modern DevOps methodologies, as shared collaborative environments introduce a high level of complexity. Requirements for standardization, security, automation, and tooling are amplified as the size of the organization grows, creating a management plane for these practices that does not exist at the individual level. Taking full advantage of these practices and conventions will increase the efficiency and velocity of any modern IT organization, providing the foresight and organizational maturity to continually assess, improve, and mature.

Index

© Oscar Medina, Ethan Schumann 2018
O. Medina and E. Schumann, *DevOps for SharePoint*, https://doi.org/10.1007/978-1-4842-3688-8